JN100534

James M. Vardaman
ジェームス・M・バーダマン
Maya Vardaman
マヤ・バーダマン

アメリカ国籍取得テストで

アメリカの一般教養と英語を学ぶ

ベレ出版

はじめに

　多くの日本人は、日常生活の中で自分の「国籍」や「市民権」（日本国民であることの権利）について考えることはあまりないかもしれません。日本人が日本人であることを改めて意識する機会は、もしかするとパスポートを取得して海外旅行に行くときくらいかもしれません。そして、「日本人としての権利」を初めて意識するのは成人になって選挙に参加するときかもしれません。

　人は自分の親が持つのと同じ国籍を、生まれながらにして自然に受け取り生活します。親の言葉を真似し、家庭や学校生活、そして社会からそれぞれの文化を自然に身につけていきます。

　日本で生まれた日本人であれば、生まれたときから自然に日本語や生活習慣を身につけ、日本の文化や歴史を学び、「日本人」になるのです。アメリカで生まれたアメリカ人も同じように、英語を学んで、アメリカの文化、歴史、社会常識を身につけ自然に「アメリカ人」になります。

　しかし、生まれた国のものではない「新しい国籍」を取得する場合もあります。

　日本以外の国籍を持つ人が日本国籍を取得しようとする場合、様々な条件を満たす必要があり、色々な書類を提出して審査を待つことになります。

　アメリカの場合も同じように様々な条件、色々な書類も準備しなければならないのですが、もう1つ違いがあります。アメリカの歴史、政治、市民の権利と責任を勉強し、テストに合格しなければなりません。当然のことながら「英語で」です。

　本書は、アメリカ社会、政府、重要な歴史的出来事、そしてほとんどのアメリカ人が学校教育や社会のなかで学んでいることに対して興味関心のある読者に向けて書かれたものです（改めてご理解いただきたいのは、本書はアメリカ国籍取得に向けて勉強する（市民権に申請する）ための学習ガイドではないということです）。

　アメリカという国が考えるアメリカ人の「常識」を楽しみながら英語で学ぶことで、英語力を高められると同時に、アメリカという国の「仕組み」や、アメリカ人の「裏」「奥」「中」を様々な角度から理解することができます。

　ここにある基礎知識を学ぶことで、アメリカ人との会話や付き合いがよりスムーズになることもあるでしょう。アメリカやアメリカ人について、新たな学びや発見を得ていただけることを願っています。

　「アメリカという国を形作る〈基盤〉は何なのか？」「アメリカ人は何を大切だと考えるのか？」を知って、〈アメリカ人になる検定試験〉のようなものに、楽しみながら挑戦してみませんか。

Give it a try!

CONTENTS

Part 1 ● アメリカの基礎知識　Basic Knowledge of the U.S.

Part 2 ● アメリカの歴史　History of the U.S.

アメリカ先住民、植民地時代と独立

近代アメリカ史：1900 年代から現在まで

Part 3 ●アメリカ政府と公民　U.S. Government and Civics

アメリカ国籍取得テスト（Citizenship Test）のことをもっと知ろう

市民権（Citizenship）って何だろう？

　日本人がアメリカを〈旅行〉する際にはパスポートがあれば OK ですが、アメリカで〈暮らす〉には、何らかの適切なビザが必要です。

　それは日本人に限ったことではなく、外国人（非市民）がアメリカで暮らすためには、「ビジネス」「学生」「難民」など、何らかのビザを持っていなければなりません。

　アメリカで暮らすことができる様々なビザの中でも、「永住権」（通称グリーンカード）は特別です。「グリーンカード」は、取得方法がいくつかあるとはいえ、狭き門であることは間違いありません。この「グリーンカード」があれば非市民でも社会保障を受けることを含め、アメリカ人とほぼ同じ資格を持てます。取得したグリーンカードを保持し続けるには、連続して 180 日以上米国外に滞在してはいけなかったり、定期的に更新を続ける必要があるなど一定のルールはありますが、それをクリアしていれば、永久に居住および仕事をすることができます。

　ただし、この「永住権」はビザの一種なので、「国籍」ではありません。グリーンカードを持っていても、「アメリカ人」ではないのです。

「市民権（Citizenship）」と「永住権（通称グリーンカード）」の違い

　では、ほぼアメリカ人と同じ資格を与えられる「永住権（グリーンカード）」と「国籍（Citizenship）」とでは、具体的に何が違うのでしょうか？

　簡単に言うと、「国籍」は更新の必要がありません。

　そして「永住権」を持っていても、アメリカでの選挙権はなく、選挙で立候補することもできません。

　逆に言うと選挙で投票する・選挙で立候補することができるのは、アメリカ国籍を持つ〈アメリカ人〉だけということです。

 アメリカ国籍を取得するには

　おそらく最も一般的な方法は、両親がアメリカ市民であるかどうかに関係なく、アメリカで生まれることです。例えば、日本人の夫婦が居住や滞在などでアメリカにいる間に子どもが生まれた場合、その子どもはアメリカの市民権（国籍）を取得する資格を持ちます。

　2つ目の方法は、出生による市民権です。アメリカ国外で生まれた場合でも、両親またはどちらかの親がアメリカ市民（アメリカ人）であれば、子どもはアメリカ市民権を取得できます。その手続きには様々な書類の提出が必要になりますが、市民権（国籍）は自動的に付帯します。

　そして3つ目の方法が、申請による取得です。申請するにはいくつかの条件を満たす必要があり、必要な書類を提出し、市民権申請面接テストに進んでいきます。この面接テストで質問される内容が、今回本書で取り上げる「アメリカの一般教養（地理・歴史・公民・生活に必要な基礎知識）」にあたります。

　ちなみに、アメリカ政府は帰化したアメリカ市民に元の市民権を保持することを認めています。つまり、もし日本人が市民権を申請し合格すれば、アメリ

カは日本のパスポートとアメリ
カのパスポートの両方を保持す
ることを認めているというわけ
です。

 ## 市民権取得の面接テストってどんなもの？

面接はアメリカ市民権取得プロセスの最終段階です。

英語で行われる一対一の面接で、まずは軽い雑談からスタートします。今日のお天気や面接会場までの交通機関についてなどの、いわゆるスモールトークなのですが、面接官からの質問に答えます。これも申請者がアメリカ社会に順応するために必要な英語力があるかを判断する材料となります。

次は、リーディングとライティングです。これは、面接官が差し出す短い文章を読み上げることと、面接官が読む内容を書きとるテストです。いずれも日本の中学で習うようなレベルのごく簡単なものです。

そして最後が本書で取り上げている「一般常識力を問う質疑応答」です。

What ocean is on the West Coast of the United States?

（アメリカの西海岸にある海は何ですか？…**地理**）

Who wrote the Declaration of Independence?

（独立宣言を書いたのは誰ですか？…**歴史**）

Who makes federal laws?

（連邦法を作るのは誰ですか？…**公民**）

Name two national U.S. holidays.

（アメリカの祝日を2つ挙げてください。…**一般常識**）

　このような、様々な内容の質問が10問出され、そのうちの6問に正解できれば合格となります。

　ここで出題される問題は、アメリカ合衆国国土安全保障省(U.S. Department of Homeland Security) の管轄である米国移民局 (U.S. Citizenship and Immigration Services) のウェブサイトにすべてサンプル問題として公表されています。"Civics (History and Government) Questions for the Naturalization Test" というファイルに出題候補100問と模範解答がすべて掲載されているので、受験者はこの100問に正しく答えられるよう、事前に勉強・準備することができるというわけです。そしてこのテストは何回でも受けることができます。

　本書の最後（p.223〜）にも100題の問題を和訳と一緒に一覧で掲載してあります。どんな問題が出るのか、まずはざっと見てみたいという方は、そちらをご覧ください。

この他には、いわゆる基本的な個人情報（住所や仕事についてなど）の確認もあるようです。

注）65歳以上、アメリカ永住権保持者として20年以上アメリカに居住している場合は、100
　問のなかの事前に指定された20問のみから10問が出題され6問正解で合格となります。
　50歳以上/20年以上の永住権保持者、55歳以上/15年以上の永住権保持者は、リスニング・
　ライティングのテストは免除されます。

 面接テストに合格すると

　指定された日に宣誓式に出席し、アメリカ国旗に向かって忠誠を誓い、晴れてアメリカ人としての国籍取得手続きが完了します。
　この宣誓式についてや、アメリカ国籍を取得したらどんな権利と義務が生じるのか？といったことについても、Citizenship Testの試験内容に含まれますので、本文でぜひご確認ください！

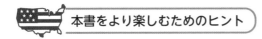

　本書を楽しみながら読み進めるために、あなたが居住する〈州〉を決めてお

くことをオススメします。面接テスト問題 100 題には、"What is the capital

of your state?（あなたが住んでいる州の州都はどこですか?）" や "Name

your U.S. Representative.（あなたの選挙区選出の下院議員の名前を挙げてく

ださい）" といった質問が含まれるためです。実際にアメリカのいずれかの州

で暮らしているイメージをしながら最新情報を調べることでも、アメリカに関

する理解が深まり、臨場感を持って本書を楽しむことができるでしょう。公職

者に関する質問には、その州の上院議員 (Senator) や下院議員 (Representative)

を調べ、その名前を用いて回答してみてください。選挙の結果によっても回答

は変わりますので、最新情報を常に確認する必要があります。

　　＊ここまでの内容は 2023 年現在の Citizenship に関する大枠を説明したものです。例外や
　　　条件の違いによって手順が異なる場合もありますので、詳細については米国移民局 (U.S.
　　　Citizenship and Immigration Services) のウェブサイトでご確認ください。
　　＊ Civics Questions には、2008 年バージョン（全 100 題）と 2020 年バージョン（全 128
　　　題）があり、以前は帰化申請した時期によってどちらのバージョンから出題されるか分か
　　　れていたのですが、現在は 2008 年バージョンへ統一する方向になっているため、本書で
　　　も 2008 年バージョンの 100 題を採用しています。
　　＊本書に掲載している解答例は "Civics (History and Government) Questions for the
　　　Naturalization Test" に記載された模範解答に準じています。

Part 1

Basic Knowledge
of the U.S.

アメリカの基礎知識

1 Land and Borders

First, let's define the geography of the U.S. It is located on the continent called North America. The contiguous 48 states (the 48 connected states excluding Alaska and Hawaii) have two international borders. On the northern border is Canada. On the southern border is Mexico.

The states on the border of Canada are: Maine, New Hampshire, Vermont, New York, Pennsylvania, Ohio, Michigan, Minnesota, North Dakota, Montana, Idaho, Washington, and Alaska.

The states on the border of Mexico are: Texas, New Mexico, Arizona, and California.

Alaska is separated from the other states by Canada. Its other border is the Pacific Ocean and the Arctic Ocean. Hawaii is a group of islands west of the other states and is surrounded by the Pacific Ocean.

Coasts :
> The Atlantic Ocean is on the East Coast of the U.S.
> The Pacific Ocean is on the West Coast of the U.S.

Let's try it!

Q89 What ocean is on the West Coast of the United States?
Q90 What ocean is on the East Coast of the United States?
Q92 Name one state that borders Canada.
Q93 Name one state that borders Mexico.

→ Answer p.45

土地と国境

　まず、アメリカの地理について説明します。アメリカは北アメリカ大陸に位置しています。陸続きで繋がっている 48 州（アラスカ州とハワイ州を除く、本土に繋がっている 48 州）には、2 つの国境があります。北の国境はカナダで、南側はメキシコです。

　カナダとの国境にある州は、メイン州、ニューハンプシャー州、バーモント州、ニューヨーク州、ペンシルベニア州、オハイオ州、ミシガン州、ミネソタ州、ノースダコタ州、モンタナ州、アイダホ州、ワシントン州、そしてアラスカ州です。

　メキシコとの国境にある州は、テキサス州、ニューメキシコ州、アリゾナ州、そしてカリフォルニア州です。

　アラスカ州はカナダによって他州から隔てられています。他の境界には太平洋と北極海があります。ハワイ州は他の州の西に位置する諸島で、太平洋に囲まれています。

海岸線：

　　大西洋はアメリカの東海岸にあります。

　　太平洋はアメリカの西海岸にあります。

Vocabulary

- ☐ geography　地理学
- ☐ contiguous　隣接の
- ☐ border　国境、領域
- ☐ be located on　～にある
- ☐ exclude　除く
- ☐ surround　囲む

17

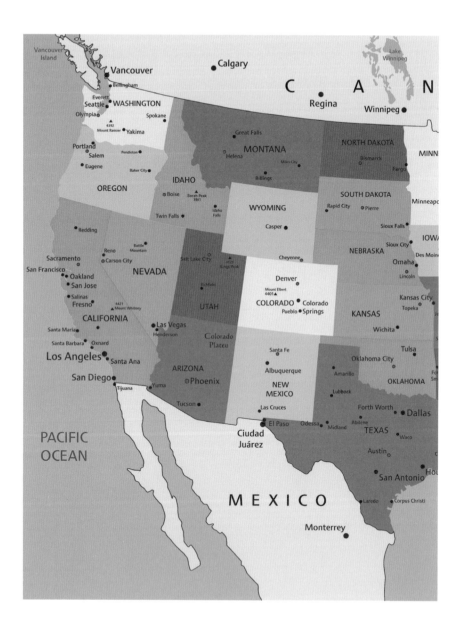

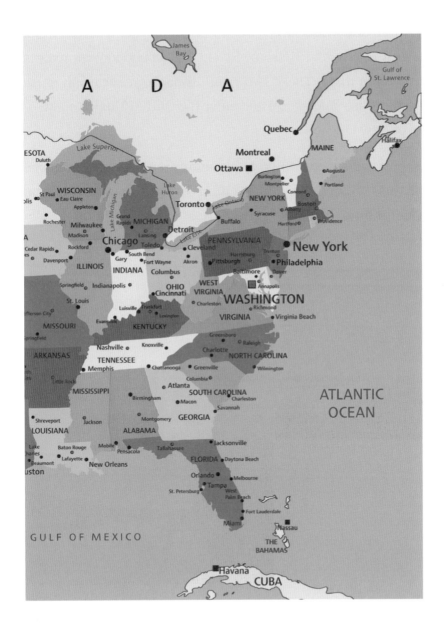

2 Rivers and Mountain Ranges

The United States is a large country and it has many large rivers. The longest river is the Missouri River. The second longest river is the Mississippi River. These two rivers come together north of St. Louis in the state of Missouri and enter the Gulf of Mexico south of the city of New Orleans.

The country has several large mountain ranges. In the eastern part of the U.S. are the Appalachian Mountains and the Blue Ridge Mountains. In the western part of the U.S. are the Rocky Mountains.

☼ *Let's try it!* ─────────────────────────────

Q 88　**Name one of the two longest rivers in the United States.**

→ Answer p.45

川と山脈

　アメリカ大陸は広く、たくさんの大きな川があります。最も長い川はミズーリ川で、次に長い川はミシシッピ川です。この2つの川はミズーリ州セントルイスの北で合流し、ニューオリンズ市の南でメキシコ湾に注ぎます。

　また、複数の大きな山脈もあります。東部にはアパラチア山脈とブルーリッジ山脈があり、西部にはロッキー山脈があります。

Vocabulary

- [ ] range　山脈
- [ ] gulf　湾
- [ ] enter　流れ込む
- [ ] several　いくつかの

3 Territories

The U.S. also has lands that are called territories. They are part of the country, but they are not states. They include the following islands and island groups:

Puerto Rico, an island in the Caribbean Sea

U.S. Virgin Islands, a group of islands between the Atlantic Ocean and the Caribbean Sea

American Samoa, a group of five islands and two atolls in the South Pacific

Northern Mariana Islands, a group of islands in the western Pacific Ocean

Guam, an island in the western Pacific Ocean

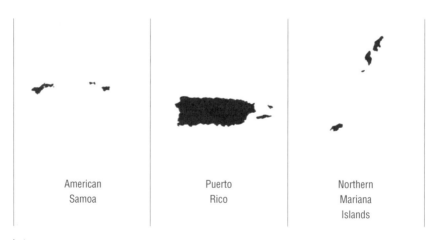

American
Samoa

Puerto
Rico

Northern
Mariana
Islands

Let's try it!

Q.91 **Name one U.S. territory.**

→ Answer p.45

米国領土

　アメリカには territories（米国領土）と呼ばれる土地もあります。これらは国の一部ではありますが、州ではありません。territories には次のような島や諸島が含まれます。

プエルトリコ（カリブ海に位置する島）

アメリカ領ヴァージン諸島（大西洋とカリブ海の間に位置する諸島）

アメリカ領サモア（南太平洋に位置する 5 つの島と 2 つのアトールからなる諸島）

北マリアナ諸島（西太平洋に位置する島々）

グアム（西太平洋に位置する島）

U.S. Virgin
Islands

Guam

Vocabulary

☐ territory　領地、準州

☐ the following　以下の

☐ atoll　環状サンゴ島

23

4 The American Flag

Each state has its own flag, but the American flag represents the whole country. The thirteen red and white stripes, representing the original thirteen colonies (the number of colonies in 1776), have not changed during America's history.

The number of the white stars on the blue background in the upper left corner has changed during our history. There is one star for each state. Until the 1950s there were 48 stars, but when Alaska and Hawaii became states, that number increased to the current 50 stars.

The flag is often called "the stars and stripes" and "the red, white, and blue."

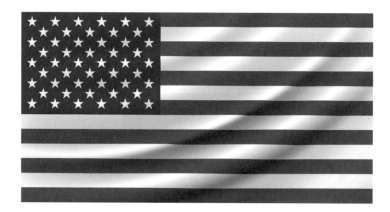

Let's try it!

Q96 Why does the flag have 13 stripes?
Q97 Why does the flag have 50 stars?

→ Answer p.45

アメリカ国旗

　各州にはそれぞれの旗がありますが、星条旗はアメリカの国全体を代表しています。13 本の赤と白のストライプは最初の 13 の植民地（1776 年にあった植民地の数）を表し、これはアメリカの歴史を通して、国旗が誕生した当初から変わっていません。

　左上の青い背景にある白い星の数は歴史を通して変わってきました。各州につき 1 つの星があります。1950 年代までは 48 の星がありましたが、アラスカとハワイが州として認定されたことにより、数が現在の 50 に増えたのです。

　この国旗はしばしば "the stars and stripes" および "the red, white, and blue" と呼ばれます。

25

5 Washington, D.C., Landmarks

The capital city, Washington, D.C., is filled with monuments, statues, and famous buildings that citizens and non-citizens can visit. The city is named after George Washington, the first president of the country. D.C. is the abbreviation for "District of Columbia," in which Columbia is a female personification of the country. Washington, D.C., is not in any state. It is a federally controlled district.

Among the impressive structures on The Mall in Washington, D.C., are the U.S. Capitol Building (known also as Capitol Hill), the Washington Monument, the Jefferson Memorial, the Lincoln Memorial, the Martin Luther King Memorial, and memorials to those who died in various wars. Facing The Mall is The White House, official residence of the President of the United States.

Let's try it!

Q94 **What is the capital of the United States?**

→ Answer p.45

ワシントン D.C. の名所

　首都のワシントン D.C. は市民、非市民にかかわらずすべての人が訪れることができるモニュメント（記念碑）、銅像や有名な建物で溢れています。この都市は初代アメリカ大統領ジョージ・ワシントンにちなんで名付けられています。D.C. は "District of Columbia（コロンビア特別区）" の略で、コロンビアはアメリカの女性擬人名です。ワシントン D.C. はどの州にも属しておらず、連邦直轄地です。

　The Mall（National Mall、ナショナルモールの通称。ワシントン D.C. の中心部に位置する国立の公園）の印象的な建造物のなかに、U.S. Capitol Building（アメリカ国会議事堂、Capitol Hill とも呼ばれる）、Washington Monument（ワシントン記念塔）、Jefferson Memorial（ジェファーソン記念館）、Lincoln Memorial（リンカーン記念堂）、Martin Luther King Memorial（マーティン・ルーサー・キング記念碑・像）、そして様々な戦争で亡くなった方々の戦没者慰霊碑があります。ホワイトハウスはナショナルモールに面しており、アメリカ合衆国大統領が居住する公邸となっています。

Vocabulary

- abbreviation　省略形
- personification　擬人化
- memorial　記念（碑、像）
- district　地区
- federally　連邦政府によって

27

6 American Symbols

America does not have a king or queen, emperor or empress, but it does have symbols of loyalty that citizens show respect to.

The Statue of Liberty is a symbol of freedom. It is in the harbor in New York City, where many immigrants once arrived in the country by ship.

Another symbol is the Liberty Bell. This one-ton iron bell was cast in 1752 in London and it hung originally in the tower of Independence Hall in Philadelphia. This building was the site of the Continental Congress that adopted the Declaration of Independence and the meeting that drafted the United States Constitution. It is said to have been rung to announce the battles of Lexington and Concord, the Declaration of Independence, and the Yorktown surrender. It developed a massive crack in 1835 and is now kept in the Liberty Bell Center pavilion.

アメリカのシンボル

アメリカには王や女王、天皇や皇后はいませんが、国民が敬意を向ける忠誠の象徴（シンボル）があります。

自由の女神は自由のシンボルです。かつて多くの移民がアメリカに来る際に船で入ってきたニューヨーク港内のリバティ島に立ちます。

もう1つのシンボルは Liberty Bell（自由の鐘）です。この1トン近くある鐘は1752年にロンドンで鋳造され、もともとフィラデルフィアの独立記念館に吊るされていました。この建物は大陸会議が独立宣言を採択し、会議で合衆国憲法を起草した場所でもあります。レキシントン・コンコードの戦いの始まり、独立宣言、そしてヨークタウンでの降伏を知らせるために鳴らされていたと言われています。1835年に大きなひびが入り、現在は（国立歴史公園内の）リバティベル・センターのパビリオンに展示されています。

Another symbol of the United States is the bald eagle, the national bird, and a symbol of freedom. It has been the national emblem of the United States since 1782.

One of many mottos of the United States: E pluribus unum, Latin for "one out of many." It stands for federal unity out of state diversity. It is the motto of the Great Seal of the United States and is used on American paper currency.

⚡ Let's try it! ───────────────────────

Q 95 Where is the Statue of Liberty?

→ Answer p.45

　ハクトウワシ（白頭鷲／ bald eagle）もアメリカのシンボルの 1 つで、国鳥でもあり、自由のシンボルでもあります。1782 年より、アメリカ合衆国の国章となっています。

　アメリカの数あるモットー（標語）の 1 つは "E pluribus unum（エ・プルリブス・ウヌム）" です。ラテン語で「多数から 1 つへ（皆ひとつになる）」という意味です。「多州から成る統一国家」を象徴します。アメリカの国章のモットーであり、アメリカ紙幣にも印刷されています。

7 Economy

The economic system of the United States is a capitalist economy. This means that the producers of most goods and services are privately owned. They are not controlled by the government. America is also a market economy. This means that the government does not decide prices of goods and services. Those prices are set by the market itself and trade is freely carried out.

One of the key locations where economic activity takes place is the New York Stock Exchange (NYSE). This is located in lower Manhattan, in New York City, and it is referred to as "Wall Street."

☀ *Let's try it!* ─────────────────────────────

　Q11　**What is the economic system in the United States?**

→ Answer p.47

アメリカの経済システムは資本主義経済です。ほとんどの商品の生産やサービスの提供は民間で担われ、政府によってコントロールされているわけではありません。また、アメリカは市場経済でもあります。つまり、政府が商品やサービスの価格を決定しません。市場そのものが価格調整を行い、取引が自由に行われるのです。

経済活動が行われる重要な場所の1つがニューヨーク証券取引所（NYSE）です。ニューヨークのマンハッタン南端の金融街にあり、このエリアは"Wall Street（ウォール街）"と呼ばれています。

Vocabulary

☐ capitalist　資本主義
☐ service　サービス（業）
☐ carry out　実行する

☐ goods　商品
☐ market economy　市場経済
☐ be referred to as　〜と言われている

8 The Pledge of Allegiance

In public schools at the beginning of the school day or the school week, students stand, face the American flag, place their right hand over their heart, and say the following pledge:

> **I pledge allegiance to the Flag**
> **of the United States of America, and to the Republic**
> **for which it stands, one Nation**
> **under God, indivisible with liberty**
> **and justice for all**

It is a pledge of loyalty to the United States and to the flag, which is a symbol of the United States.

The pledge originally appeared in a magazine for young people in 1892, which was the 400th anniversary of Christopher Columbus's discovery of America. It was used in public schools on Columbus Day that year as a 15-second pledge of loyalty to the United States. As an aside, the phrase "under God" was not added until 1954, and in that year the pledge was made official by a government bill signed by President Eisenhower.

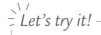 *Let's try it!*

Q52 **What do we show loyalty to when we say the Pledge of Allegiance?**

→ Answer p.47

忠誠宣誓

　公立の学校での 1 日や 1 週間の始まりに、生徒は星条旗に向かって起立し、右手を胸にあてて以下の宣誓を唱えます：

　私はアメリカ合衆国の国旗と、

　その国旗が象徴する共和国、

　神のもとで、すべての人々に自由と正義が約束された、

　分かつことのできない 1 つの国に忠誠を誓います。

　これはアメリカ合衆国、そしてアメリカのシンボルである国旗に対して忠誠を表す誓いです。

　この宣誓は、クリストファー・コロンブスのアメリカ大陸発見から 400 周年記念であった 1892 年に、若者向けの雑誌に初めて登場しました。その年のコロンブス・デーに、公立学校で 15 秒のアメリカ合衆国への忠誠の誓いとして使われました。ところで、"under God（神のもとで）" の部分は 1954 年まで加わっておらず、その年にアイゼンハワー大統領が法案に署名したことによって正式な文言になりました。

Vocabulary

- ☐ pledge　宣誓、誓う
- ☐ stand (for)　～を表す
- ☐ liberty　自由
- ☐ official　公的な
- ☐ allegiance　忠誠
- ☐ indivisible　分割できない
- ☐ aside　余談

9 The National Anthem

The lyrics of the National Anthem were composed by Francis Scott Key during the War of 1812. We call that song "The Star-Spangled Banner" and the first stanza is:

Oh, say, can you see by the dawn's early light,

What so proudly we hailed at the twilight's last gleaming?

Whose broad stripes and bright stars, through the perilous fight,

O'er the ramparts we watched were so gallantly streaming?

And the rockets' red glare, the bombs bursting in air,

Gave proof through the night that our flag was still there.

Oh, says, does that star-spangled banner yet wave

O'er the land of the free and the home of the brave?

The National Anthem is often sung at public gatherings and is sometimes played at the beginning of sports events. We stand, put our right hand over our heart, and sing it together.

Let's try it!

Q 98 What is the name of the national anthem?

国歌

　国家の歌詞は、1812 年の戦争（米英戦争）中に、作曲家のフランシス・スコット・キーによって書かれました。"The Star-Spangled Banner（輝く星条旗）"と呼ばれており、最初の一節は以下の通りです：

おお見えん、黎明の光に照らされて

誇り高く　たそがれの最後の輝きに　我らが称えしものが

その縞模様と輝く星　危険な戦いを通じて

防御の砦のかなたに我らが見し　その光が勇敢にも差し込むのを

大砲の紅連の輝き　空に炸裂する爆弾

そこに　我らの旗が　夜を徹してののち　いまだそこなわれざるを

ああ　星条旗はまだはためいているか

自由の大地　勇者の故郷の上に

　国歌はしばしば公共の集まりやスポーツイベントの冒頭で歌われます。起立し、右手を胸にあて、共に歌います。

Vocabulary

- ☐ national anthem　国歌
- ☐ twilight　夕暮れ
- ☐ ramparts　城壁
- ☐ stanza　節
- ☐ gleaming　輝き、閃光
- ☐ banner　旗

10 National Holidays

Another kind of national symbol is a federal holiday. Some of these days represent or honor a person or an event in our country's history.

 New Year's Day (January 1)

 Martin Luther King, Jr., Day (the third Monday in January) honors Dr. Martin Luther King, Jr., who worked hard to see that all people were treated fairly.

Presidents' Day (the third Monday in February) honors all of those who served as President of the United States. It was originally a celebration of George Washington's birthday.

Memorial Day (the last Monday of May) is for mourning the United States military personnel who died while serving in the Armed Forces. At national cemeteries, people place flowers and American flags on graves of military personnel. Initially it was called Decoration Day, a time for decorating the graves of Civil War soldiers. It now commemorates all those who died in all wars.

連邦祝日も国のシンボルの1つです。なかには国の歴史上の人物や出来事を象徴したり称えたりする日もあります。

☆ 元日（1月1日）

☆ マーティン・ルーサー・キング牧師の日（1月の第3月曜日）は、すべての人が公平に扱われるよう尽力したマーティン・ルーサー・キング・ジュニア博士を称える（生誕を記念する）日です。

☆ 大統領の日（2月の第3月曜日）は、歴代のアメリカ大統領を記念する（称える）日です。もともとは初代大統領のジョージ・ワシントンの生誕記念日でした。

☆ メモリアル・デー［戦没将兵追悼記念日］（5月の最終月曜日）は、軍隊で兵役中に亡くなった方々を追悼する日です。国立墓地では亡くなった方々のお墓にお花やアメリカの国旗を飾ります。最初は「デコレーション・デー」と呼ばれ、南北戦争の兵士のお墓を飾る日でした。現在は、戦争で亡くなったすべての方々を追悼する日となっています。

JUN 19 **Juneteenth** (June 19) became a Texas state holiday in 1980 and a federal holiday in 2021. It commemorates the freeing of slaves at the end of the Civil War. It was not until June 19, 1865, that Union General Gordon Granger told the slaves in Galveston, Texas, that they were free. President Lincoln announced the Emanicipation Proclamation on September 22, 1862, but it was three years before the slaves there learned that they were free.

JUL 04 **Independence Day** (July 4) is also called "The Fourth of July." It celebrates the independence of the American colonies from Britain in 1776. It is known as the country's birthday, because it is the day that the Declaration of Independence was signed.

 Labor Day (the first Monday in September) celebrates workers and how they contribute to America.

OCT Second MON **Columbus Day** (the second Monday in October) officially celebrates Christopher Columbus's arrival in the Americas on the shores of the Bahamas in 1492. Some states do not observe this holiday. Other states call this "Indigenous People's Day." Hawaii calls it "Discoverers' Day" and South Dakota calls it "Native American Day." Many Italian-Americans celebrate their heritage rather than Columbus himself on that day.

☆ ジューンティーンス（6月19日）は1980年にテキサス州の祝日になり、2021年に連邦祝日となりました。南北戦争終結時の奴隷解放を記念する日です。1865年6月19日、北軍のゴードン・グレンジャー将軍がテキサス州ガルベストンで奴隷の解放を告げました。奴隷制の最終的な終わりを意味しますが、それは1862年9月22日にリンカーン大統領が奴隷解放宣言を出してから約3年後のことでした。

☆ **独立記念日**（7月4日）は"The Fourth of July（ザ・フォース・オブ・ジュライ）"とも呼ばれます。1776年に植民地がイギリスから独立を果たしたことを祝います。独立宣言が採択された日であるため、建国記念日としても知られています。

☆ レイバー・デー［労働祭］（9月の第1月曜日）は、労働者に敬意を示し、アメリカへの貢献を称える日です。

☆ コロンブス・デー（10月の第2月曜日）は、1492年のクリストファー・コロンブスのアメリカ大陸（正確にはバハマの海岸）への上陸を祝う法定祝日です。州によってはこの日を祝日としていません。また、"Indigenous People's Day（アメリカ先住民の日）"と呼び、この日を祝う州もあります。ハワイ州では"Discoverers' Day（発見者たちの日）"と呼び、サウスダコタ州では"Native American Day（ネイティブ・アメリカン・デー）"と呼んでいます。多くのイタリア系アメリカ人はこの日に、コロンブス本人のことよりも自分たちの伝統を祝います。

NOV 11 **Veterans Day** (November 11) is a federal holiday for honoring military veterans of the United States Armed Forces. It coincides with other holidays in Europe such as Armistice Day—later renamed Remembrance Day—that mark the anniversary of the end of World War I. November 11, 1918, was the day when the Armistice with Germany went into effect. It also honors people currently serving in the military.

NOV Fourth THU **Thanksgiving Day** (the fourth Thursday in November) celebrates the day in 1621 when the Pilgrims in Plymouth colony gave thanks for the good things they had in America. Together with the Native Americans, they had a great feast, a big dinner. Since that time, Americans have invited family and friends to gather and share a big dinner. They often eat turkey, cranberry sauce, corn, squash and sweet potatoes, like the Native Americans taught the Pilgrims to grow and cook. The day after Thanksgiving Day is also a holiday, so the four-day weekend is a major traveling day around the country.

DEC 25 **Christmas Day** (December 25)

Let's try it!

Q99 When do we celebrate Independence Day?

Q100 Name two national U.S. holidays.

→ Answer p.47

☆ ベテランズ・デー［退役軍人の日、復員軍人の日］（11月11日）は、アメリカの軍の人々を称える連邦祝日です。ヨーロッパで祝われる第一次世界大戦の終戦を記念する日（"Armistice Day"、後に "Remembrance Day" に変更）と同じ日です。1918年11月11日にドイツとの休戦協定が締結されたのです。今現在、軍務に就いている人々を称える日でもあります。

☆ サンクスギビング・デー［感謝祭］（11月の第4木曜日）は、1621年にプリマス植民地のピルグリム（「巡礼者」の意味）がアメリカでの恵みに感謝した日を記念して祝う日です。ピルグリムたちはネイティブ・アメリカンと晩餐を共にしました。それ以来、アメリカ人は夕食に家族や友人を招待して一緒に豪華な食事をとるようになりました。食卓によく並ぶのはターキー、クランベリーソース、コーン、カボチャ、さつまいも（ヤムいも）で、これらはネイティブ・アメリカンがピルグリムに作物作りから料理法まで、作り方を教えた品々です。サンクスギビング・デーの翌日も祝日なので、4連休の週末は全国で多くの人々が移動をします。

☆ クリスマス（12月25日）

Vocabulary

□ honor　栄光を与える
□ mourn　悲しむ、追悼する
□ heritage　伝統、遺産

□ celebration　祭典、礼賀
□ commemorate　記念する、祝う

Let's Try Test Questions

Page 16

Q 89 What ocean is on the West Coast of the United States?

Q 90 What ocean is on the East Coast of the United States?

Q 92 Name one state that borders Canada.

Q 93 Name one state that borders Mexico.

Page 20

Q 88 Name one of the two longest rivers in the United States.

Page 22

Q 91 Name one U.S. territory.

Page 24

Q 96 Why does the flag have 13 stripes?

Q 97 Why does the flag have 50 stars?

Page 26

Q 94 What is the capital of the United States?

Page 30

Q 95 Where is the Statue of Liberty?

Answers

A 89 アメリカの西海岸にある海は何ですか？
Pacific (Ocean) パシフィック（オーシャン）、太平洋

A 90 アメリカの東海岸にある海は何ですか？
Atlantic (Ocean) アトランティック（オーシャン）、大西洋

A 92 カナダと国境を接している州を1つ挙げてください。
Maine メイン州，**New Hampshire** ニューハンプシャー州，**Vermont** バーモント州，**New York** ニューヨーク州，**Pennsylvania** ペンシルベニア州，**Ohio** オハイオ州，**Michigan** ミシガン州，**Minnesota** ミネソタ州，**North Dakota** ノースダコタ州，**Montana** モンタナ州，**Idaho** アイダホ州，**Washington** ワシントン州，**Alaska** アラスカ州

A 93 メキシコと国境を接している州を1つ挙げてください。
California カリフォルニア州，**Arizona** アリゾナ州，**New Mexico** ニューメキシコ州，**Texas** テキサス州

A 88 アメリカで最も長い川の2つのうち1つを挙げてください。
Missouri (River) ミズーリ（川），**Mississippi (River)** ミシシッピ（川）

A 91 アメリカの領土を1つ挙げてください。
Puerto Rico プエルトリコ，**U.S. Virgin Islands** アメリカ領ヴァージン諸島，**American Samoa** アメリカ領サモア，**Northern Mariana Islands** 北マリアナ諸島，**Guam** グアム

A 96 国旗に13本のストライプがある理由は何ですか？
Because there were 13 original colonies. （独立当初に）13の植民地があったため，**Because the stripes represent the original colonies.** ストライプは13植民地を表すため

A 97 国旗に50個の星がある理由は何ですか？
Because there is one star for each state. 各州につき1つの星があるため，**Because each star represents a state.** 星が州を表しているため，**Because there are 50 states.** 50州あるため

A 94 アメリカの首都はどこですか？
Washington, D.C. ワシントン D.C.

A 95 自由の女神像はどこにありますか？
New York (Harbor) ニューヨーク（港），**Liberty Island** リバティ島，**New Jersey** ニュージャージー州，**near New York City** ニューヨーク市近辺，**on the Hudson (River)** ハドソン（川）

A11 アメリカ合衆国の経済体制は何ですか？
Capitalist economy 資本主義経済，**Market economy** 市場経済

A52 忠誠宣誓を唱える際、何に対して忠誠を誓うのですか？
The United States アメリカ合衆国，**The flag**（アメリカの）国旗

A98 国歌の名前は何ですか？
The Star-Spangled Banner（輝く星条旗）

A99 独立記念日はいつですか？
July 4, The Fourth of July 7月4日

A100 アメリカの祝日を2つ挙げてください。
New Year's Day 元日，**Martin Luther King, Jr., Day** マーティン・ルーサー・キング牧師の日，**Presidents' Day** 大統領の日，**Memorial Day** メモリアル・デー，**Juneteenth** ジューンティーンス，**Independence Day** 独立記念日，**Labor Day** レイバー・デー，**Columbus Day** コロンブス・デー，**Veterans Day** ベテランズ・デー，**Thanksgiving Day** サンクスギビング・デー，**Christmas Day** クリスマス

Head of the Statue of Liberty on display at Champ-de-Mars,
Exposition Universelle, Paris, 1878

Part 2

History
of the U.S.

アメリカの歴史

The First Americans

Children often learn that Columbus "discovered" America, but that is not true. There were already people living there before he and other Europeans came. Columbus mistakenly called these people "Indians." But today we call them Native Americans or American Indians.

Today there are 562 federally recognized tribes of American Indians and Alaska Natives in the U.S. They have their own tribal governments.

Among the well-known tribes are the following:

Apache	Arawak	Blackfeet	Cherokee
Cheyenne	Chippewa	Choctaw	Creek
Crow	Hopi	Huron	Inuit
Iroquois	Lakota	Mohegan	Navajo
Oneida	Onondaga	Pueblo	Seminole
Seneca	Shawnee	Sioux	Teton

Let's try it!

Q59 Who lived in America before the Europeans arrived?

Q87 Name one American Indian tribe in the United States.

→ Answer p.73

最初のアメリカ人

子どもたちは、コロンブスがアメリカを「発見した」と教わりますが、実はそれは正確ではありません。コロンブスをはじめ他のヨーロッパ人が到着する前からそこには人々が住んでいました。コロンブスは誤ってその人々のことを「インディアン」と呼びました。しかし、現在は「ネイティブ・アメリカン」または「アメリカン・インディアン」と呼びます。

現在、アメリカには562の連邦政府公認のアメリカン・インディアンおよびアラスカ先住民の部族が存在し、それぞれ部族政府を持っています。

よく知られている部族は次の通りです：

アパッチ	アラワク	ブラックフット	チェロキー
シャイアン	チペワ	チョクトー	クリーク
クロウ	ホピ	ヒューロン	イヌイット
イロコイ	ラコタ	モヘガン	ナバホ
オナイダ	オノンダガ	プエブロ	セミノール
セネカ	ショーニー	スー	テトン

Vocabulary

- [ ] mistakenly　間違って、考え違いに
- [ ] tribal　部族の
- [ ] recognize　（公式に）認める
- [ ] well-known　広く知られている

2 The Colonists

The people from Europe who first came to America in the 1600s were mostly from England. However, there were also people from Holland, France, Germany, and Scandinavia. These people were called "colonists." The communities they formed were called "colonies."

The colonists came to America for various reasons. Some sought to escape from persecution for religious and political reasons. They wanted freedom and political liberty. Others sought religious freedom. They wanted to be able to practice their religion freely. Still others sought economic opportunity, which they did not have in their former countries.

Let's try it!

Q58 **What is one reason colonists came to America?**

→ Answer p.73

　1600 年代に初めてヨーロッパからアメリカに来た人々のほとんどはイギリスから渡ってきました。しかし、オランダ、フランス、ドイツおよびスカンジナビアからの人々もいました。彼らは "colonists（入植者）" と呼ばれ、彼らが形成したコミュニティは "colonies（コロニー）" と呼ばれました。

　その人々がアメリカに渡った理由は様々でした。宗教や政治的な理由による迫害（抑圧）から逃れようとした者もいました。政治的自由を求めたり、自由に宗教を信仰するための宗教的な自由を求める人々もいました。また、他にも自国ではなかった経済的なチャンスを求める人々もいました。

Vocabulary

☐ colonist　植民地開拓者、入植者
☐ sought（seek の過去形）　求めた
☐ political liberty　政治的自由
☐ community　コミュニティ、地域社会
☐ persecution　迫害
☐ former　以前の

3 The First Colonies

The first colony was in Jamestown, Virginia. These colonists arrived in 1607 and they came to America for economic opportunities. They raised various crops to sell in trade with England. The first crops included indigo and rice. The first successful crop was tobacco, which became popular in England and other European countries.

The second British colony was in Plymouth, Massachusetts. The colonists there arrived in 1620 and the people were Pilgrims, who were not free to practice their religion in England and freely follow their religious beliefs. These are the people that sailed on the ship called the *Mayflower*. In 1629, another group called the Puritans came for freedom to create a new church in America.

Jamestown and Vicinity.

　最初の植民地はバージニア州ジェームズタウンにありました。ジェームズタウンの入植者たちは1607年に経済的チャンスを求めてアメリカにやってきました。彼らは様々な作物を育て、イギリスと貿易をしました。最初の作物のなかにはインディゴ（インド藍）と米がありました。最初に成功した作物はタバコで、イギリスや他のヨーロッパの国々で人気となりました。

　第2のイギリス植民地はマサチューセッツ州プリマスでした。入植者はピルグリムで、1620年に信仰の自由を求めてやってきました。ピルグリムたちはイギリスでは信仰を貫くことが叶わなかったのです。彼らがメイフラワー号でやってきた人たちです。1629年には、ピューリタンという別の集団がアメリカに新しい教会を建てる自由を求めてやってきました。

Vocabulary

☐ crop　作物、収穫物　　　　　　☐ indigo　インディゴ（インド藍）
☐ Pilgrim　ピルグリム・ファーザーズの一員

4 How the Colonies Developed

Virginia was in what we call the South. The colonists there found it was hard work to grow crops like tobacco and they brought laborers from England to cut down forests and make new fields. But there were not enough of these laborers to do the work. The colonists then began to buy slaves from Africa to do the work. These African slaves worked on plantations, where they were treated cruelly. The owners of the plantations, however, became wealthy and controlled the local governments.

Massachusetts was in what we call the North. The colonists there lived in small villages, where some were farmers and others became craftspeople. There were also some slaves, but not as many as in the South.

Let's try it!

> **Q60** What group of people was taken to America and sold as slaves?

→ Answer p.73

植民地の発展

　バージニア州は"the South（南部）"と呼ばれる地域にありました。そこの入植者たちは、タバコなどの作物を育てるのは大変な労力が必要だとわかると、イギリスから労働者を連れてきて、森林の木を切り倒し、新しく畑を作らせました。ただ、十分な労働者の数がなく、入植者たちは作業をさせるためにアフリカから奴隷を買い取り始めました。アフリカの奴隷たちはプランテーション（大農場）で働き、残酷な扱いを受けました。一方で、プランテーションの所有者は裕福になり、地方自治体を統治するようになりました。

　マサチューセッツ州は"the North（北部）"と呼ばれる地域にありました。そこの入植者たちは小さな集落に住み、農民もいれば、職人になった人もいました。奴隷もいましたが、南部ほど多くはいませんでした。

Tobacco

Vocabulary

☐ laborer　労働者
☐ plantation　プランテーション
☐ craftspeople　職人

☐ slave　奴隷
☐ treat　扱う

5 Differences Between North and South

The colonists in the North and South developed different ideas.

Northern colonists wanted to be free to trade and do business without being taxed by the British government. The government in England expected the colonists to be loyal, pay taxes, and not trade with other countries. The Northern colonists also wanted the Southern colonists to buy goods from the North, rather than buying British goods.

Southern colonists wanted to sell the tobacco, indigo, rice, and cotton directly to Britain and buy goods directly from Britain. They did not want to be tied to the Northern colonists and pay high prices for products from Northern factories.

北部と南部の違い

北と南の入植者たちはそれぞれ異なった考えを培っていました。

北部の入植者たちは、イギリス政府から課税されずに、自由に貿易や事業が行えることを望んでいました。イギリス政府は、入植者が忠誠心を持ち、税金を払い、他の国と貿易をしないことを求めました。北部の入植者たちは、南部の入植者たちにイギリスの商品ではなく北部の商品を買ってほしかったのです。

南部の入植者たちは、タバコ、インディゴ（インド藍）、米、そして綿花を直接イギリスに売り、イギリスから商品を直接買うことを望んでいました。北部の入植者たちに縛られ、北部の工場の商品に高額を支払うことを避けたかったのです。

Vocabulary

☐ tax　課税する

☐ be tied to　〜に縛り付けられる

☐ goods　商品

☐ factory　工場

6 Agreements Between the Colonies

Although the colonies of the North and South disagreed about many things, they agreed that they wanted to make their own decisions, have their own government, and not have to pay heavy taxes to Britain.

The leaders of the colonies disliked several things about the way the British government treated them.

First, they disliked having to pay high taxes to the British government.

Second, they did not like being taxed without having any representation in the British Parliament.

Third, they disliked being required to board and quarter British soldiers. This meant that the British army soldiers lived in their houses and ate meals without paying anything.

Fourth, they did not have self-government. All of the laws they had to follow were established on the other side of the Atlantic Ocean—in Britain.

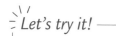

Let's try it!

Q61 Why did the colonists fight the British?

→ Answer p.73

植民地間の協定

　北部と南部の植民地は多くのことで意見が対立していましたが、自らが物事を決断し、政府を持ち、イギリスに多額の税金を支払うことは避けたいという点では意見が一致していました。

　植民地の指導者たちは、イギリス政府による扱いに対していくつかの不満を持っていました。

　　1つ目は、イギリス政府に高額の税金を払わなければいけないことでした。
　　2つ目は、課税されているにもかかわらず、イギリス議会に代表を送れないことでした。
　　3つ目は、イギリス兵に食料と居住の提供を求められていることでした。イギリス軍の兵士は何も支払わずに入植者の家に居住し、食事をしていたのです。
　　4つ目は、自治がなかったことでした。入植者が従うべき法律はすべて大西洋を渡った反対側、つまりイギリスで定められていたのです。

Vocabulary

- [ ] although　〜とはいえ
- [ ] be required to　〜を要求される
- [ ] dislike　嫌がる、好まない
- [ ] self-government　自治

7 The Colonies Break with Britain

The American colonists were unable to agree with many of the decisions that were made in Britain about how the colonies should be governed. A number of events occurred that emphasized the colonists' unhappiness with their situation. A few of the main events are mentioned below.

① The Stamp Act

In 1765, the British government passed a law that required the payment of a tax on a wide variety of papers and documents, including newspapers, in the American colonies. Special stamps were attached to these papers to show that the tax had been paid. This Stamp Act created the first direct tax on the Americans, who strongly protested. The American colonists petitioned King George III to repeal the act, and he did so the following year.

植民地とイギリスの決別

アメリカの植民地人たちは、イギリスが定めた植民地の統治方法について、ほとんど同意することができませんでした。植民地人たちの状況への不満を際立たせるような出来事がいくつも起きました。そのうちの主な出来事を次に紹介します。

① 印紙税法

イギリス政府は 1765 年、アメリカの植民地を対象に、新聞を含む幅広い紙や文書に税の支払いを義務付ける法律を制定しました。これらの紙類には税金が支払われたことを証明する特別な切手が貼られました。この印紙税法はアメリカ人に課せられた初の直接税で、彼らは強く抗議しました。アメリカの植民地人は国王ジョージ 3 世にこの法律を廃止するよう請願し、翌年、この法律は廃止されました。

Vocabulary

☐ break with　〜と決別する
☐ emphasize　強調する
☐ document　文書、書類
☐ be unable to　〜できない
☐ payment　支払い
☐ repeal　撤回する、廃止する

② The Townshend Acts

The British parliament passed the Townshend Acts in 1767 to place duties on imports into the American colonies. The four acts placed duties on imports of paint, glass, paper, tea, and lead. They established a board of customs agents to enforce the collection of these duties. The colonists protested these new measures as "taxation without representation." The Americans believed that the government in Britain had no right to make all of the laws that affected the American colonies.

③ The Boston Massacre

In a clash between British troops and townspeople in Boston in 1770, the British fired into a crowd that was threatening them.

The soldiers had been sent to help the government maintain order. The British soldiers were resented even before this incident, which is known as the Boston Massacre. Five colonists were killed, including a Black sailor named Crispus Attucks. It is said that he was one of the first Americans to die in the struggle for liberty.

② タウンゼンド諸法

イギリス議会は 1767 年、アメリカ植民地への輸入品に関税を課するタウンゼンド諸法を可決しました。この 4 つの法令は、塗料、ガラス、紙、茶、そして鉛の輸入に関税を課したものです。また、これらの関税の徴収を強化するために関税局が設立されました。これらの新しい法案に対し、植民地の人々は「代表なき課税」だとして抗議しました。アメリカ人は、イギリス政府にはアメリカの植民地に影響する法律を制定する権利はないと考えていたのです。

③ ボストン大虐殺

1770 年、ボストンでイギリス軍と植民地人との間で衝突が起き、イギリス兵は威嚇してきた群集に向けて発砲しました。その兵士たちは、政府が治安を維持するための護衛として派遣されていました。植民地人は兵士たちに対してこの事件の前から憤慨していました。これが「ボストン大虐殺」として知られる事件です。5 人の植民地人が殺され、そのなかにはクリスパス・アタックスという名の黒人水兵も含まれていました。彼は自由のための闘いで亡くなった最初のアメリカ人の 1 人だと言われています。

Vocabulary

☐ parliament （イギリス）議会
☐ protest 抗議する
☐ troops 軍
☐ struggle 奮闘する、苦心する
☐ duty 関税
☐ massacre 大虐殺
☐ resent 憤る、憤慨する

④ The Boston Tea Party

In 1773, the British government in London gave a British company the right to sell tea directly to the colonies in America. This undercut American tea merchants. A group of colonists found a ship in Boston Harbor that was loaded with the company's tea. They dressed up as American Indians, boarded the ship, and threw hundreds of chests of tea overboard into the water. The event became known as the Boston Tea Party. The British government tried to punish the colonists by closing Boston as a port, but this only made the colonists resist the rule of the British king even further.

These and other events led the leaders of the American colonies to decide to break completely with Britain and become independent.

④ ボストン茶会事件

1773 年、ロンドンにあるイギリス政府は、イギリスのある貿易会社にアメリカの植民地に直接紅茶を販売する権利を与えました。すると、アメリカの紅茶の商人たちよりも安い価格で販売したのです。植民地人数名がボストン港でこの会社の紅茶を積んだ船を見つけました。彼らはアメリカン・インディアンの装いで船に乗り込み、数百もの茶箱をボストン港に投げ込みました。この事件は「ボストン茶会事件」として知られるようになったのです。イギリス政府はボストン港を閉鎖し、植民地人を罰しようとしましたが、これは植民地人のイギリス国王による支配に対する反発を強めただけでした。

こういった一連の事件により、アメリカ植民地の指導者たちはイギリスと完全に決別し、独立することを決意したのです。

Vocabulary

☐ undercut　安く売る
☐ overboard　船外に
☐ resist　反抗する、抵抗する

☐ load　載せる、積む
☐ punish　罰する

8 The Continental Congress

Delegates from the thirteen colonies gathered in the Continental Congress for the first time in 1774. When it reconvened in 1775, it organized for war against Britain, and eventually signed the Declaration of Independence. The Congress served as the main connection between the colonies after they declared their independence as states. Much later, the Congress approved an agreement, in 1782, that provided for a loose federal government between the original thirteen states.

Carpenters Hall (Philadelphia), where the Continental Congress was held

　1774 年、13 の植民地の代表者が初めて大陸会議と呼ばれる会合のために集まりました。1775 年に再び招集した際には、会議はイギリスとの戦争のために組織され、その後、独立宣言に調印しました。植民地が州として独立を宣言した後も、議会は植民地同士をつなぐ重要な役割を担いました。後に、1782 年には連邦議会が 13 の州にゆるい形での連邦政府を設立する協定を承認しました。

Vocabulary

- [ ] reconvene　再召集する
- [ ] declare　宣言する、公告する
- [ ] loose　ゆるい
- [ ] eventually　ついには
- [ ] provide　設立する

9 The Declaration of Independence

After long discussions between the delegates of the Congress, they signed a document that was written mainly by Thomas Jefferson. They adopted the Declaration of Independence on July 4, 1776. That is why Americans celebrate that day as Independence Day. They usually call that day "The Fourth of July."

The Declaration of Independence explained the reasons for separation from Britain and gave the principles for forming a new government in America. One important passage in the Declaration is as follows:

> **We hold these truths to be self-evident: that all men are created equal; that they are endowed by their creator with certain unalienable rights; that among these are life, liberty, and the pursuit of happiness...**

The Declaration says that all people are created equal, they have certain specific rights, and they have individual freedom.

Let's try it!

Q 8 What did the Declaration of Independence do?

Q 9 What are two rights in the Declaration of Independence?

Q 62 Who wrote the Declaration of Independence?

Q 63 When was the Declaration of Independence adopted?

→ Answer p.73

　長時間におよぶ議論の後、議会の代表者は、トーマス・ジェファーソンが中心となって書かれた文書に署名しました。1776年7月4日、彼らは独立宣言を採択したのです。これが、アメリカ人がこの日を独立記念日として祝う背景です。彼らは普段、その日のことを"The Fourth of July（ザ・フォース・オブ・ジュライ）"と呼びます。

　独立宣言はイギリスから分離した理由を述べ、アメリカで新しい政府を設立するための原則について記しています。宣言にある重要な一節には次のように書かれています：

> **われわれは、次のことが自明の真理であると信ずる。すべての人は平等に創られ、創造主によって一定の奪われることのない権利を与えられていること。そのなかには生命、自由、幸福の追求が含まれていること。**

　この宣言は、すべての人は平等に創られ、特定の権利を持ち、個人の自由を持っていると述べているのです。

Vocabulary

- □ declaration　宣言
- □ principle　基本方針、原則
- □ unalienable　譲渡できない
- □ separation　分離
- □ passage　（文書の）一節

Let's Try Test Questions

Page 50

Q 59 Who lived in America before the Europeans arrived?

Q 87 Name one American Indian tribe in the United States.

Page 52

Q 58 What is one reason colonists came to America?

Page 56

Q 60 What group of people was taken to America and sold as slaves?

Page 60

Q 61 Why did the colonists fight the British?

Page 70

Q 8 What did the Declaration of Independence do?

Q 9 What are two rights in the Declaration of Independence?

Q 62 Who wrote the Declaration of Independence?

Q 63 When was the Declaration of Independence adopted?

Answers

A 59 ヨーロッパ人が到着する前のアメリカには誰が住んでいましたか？
American Indians アメリカン・インディアン，**Native Americans** ネイティブ・アメリカン

A 87 アメリカ先住民の部族名を1つ挙げてください。
Cherokee チェロキー，**Navajo** ナバホ，**Sioux** スー，**Chippewa** チペワ，**Choctaw** チョクトー，**Pueblo** プエブロ，**Apache** アパッチ，**Iroquois** イロコイ，**Creek** クリーク，**Blackfeet** ブラックフット，**Seminole** セミノール，**Cheyenne** シャイアン，**Arawak** アラワク，**Shawnee** ショーニー，**Mohegan** モヘガン，**Huron** ヒューロン，**Oneida** オナイダ，**Lakota** ラコタ，**Crow** クロウ，**Teton** テトン，**Hopi** ホピ，**Inuit** イヌイット

A 58 入植者がアメリカに来た理由の1つを挙げてください。
Freedom 自由のため，**Political liberty** 政治的(抑圧からの)自由のため，**Religious freedom** 信教の自由のため，**Economic opportunity** 経済的な機会を得るため，**Practice their religion** 宗教を信仰するため，**Escape persecution** 迫害から逃れるため

A 60 アメリカへ連れ去られて奴隷として売られたのはどのような人々ですか？
Africans アフリカの人々，**People from Africa** アフリカ出身者

A 61 入植者はなぜイギリスと戦ったのですか？
Because of high taxes (taxation without representation) 税金が高額なため(代表なき課税)，**Because the British army stayed in their houses (boarding, quartering)** イギリス軍が彼らの家に滞在したため(寄宿、宿営)，**Because they didn't have self-government** 自治がなかったため

A 8 独立宣言は何をしましたか？
Announced our independence (from Great Britain) (イギリスの支配からの)独立を発表した，**Declared our independence (from Great Britain)** (イギリスの支配からの)独立を宣言した，**Said that the United States is free (from Great Britain)** アメリカは(イギリスの支配から)自由だと述べた

A 9 独立宣言に述べられている権利を2つ挙げてください。
Life 生命，**Liberty** 自由，**Pursuit of happiness** 幸福の追求

A 62 独立宣言を書いたのは誰ですか？
(Thomas) Jefferson (トーマス)ジェファーソン

A 63 独立宣言が採択されたのはいつですか？
July 4, 1776 1776年7月4日

10 The American Revolution

① Battles at Lexington and Concord

The colonists stored weapons at Concord, Massachusetts, west of Boston. When British troops were sent to capture the weapons, they were confronted by a band of colonists. They were called "minutemen" because they could be ready to fight within minutes.

The first fighting began in the town of Lexington, but the British continued on to Concord. They did not find a large store of supplies, but the minutemen attacked them and followed the British troops all the way back to Boston. This battle is considered the beginning of the American Revolution.

アメリカ独立戦争

① レキシントン・コンコードの戦い

　植民地人たちは、ボストンの西に位置するマサチューセッツ州のコンコードに武器を保管していました。イギリス軍がその武器を没収しに派遣された際、植民地人（植民地軍）が抵抗し、衝突したのです。この植民地人は民兵で、数分以内で戦闘態勢につけることから "minutemen（ミニットメン）" と呼ばれました。

　独立戦争の最初の戦いはレキシントンの町で始まり、イギリス軍はコンコードまで進みました。そこでは多くの軍事物資は発見されませんでしたが、ミニットメンは彼らを攻撃し、ボストンまでイギリス軍を追って戻りました。この戦いがアメリカ独立戦争の始まりだとされています。

Vocabulary

- [ ] store　保管する、蓄積する
- [ ] confront　対抗する
- [ ] weapon　武器
- [ ] be considered　〜と考えられている

② Washington Crossing the Delaware River (Battle of Trenton)

One of the major battles of the war took place when the colonists deeded a real victory. The British hired German (Hessian) troops to fight against the colonists. On Christmas night, December 25, 1776, these troops were camped at the town of Trenton, New Jersey. In the cold darkness, General George Washington and his troops crossed over the icy Delaware River and attacked the resting Hessians, killing or capturing two thirds of them. This victory encouraged the American colonists.

③ The Battle of Saratoga

The British planned to send thousands of troops from Canada into the colonies to capture the New England states and split the colonies in half. The British were well supplied when they left Canada. On the other hand, the American soldiers were half-starved and had poor clothes and equipment.

But as the British moved south, they were delayed by American attacks and began to run out of food, supplies, and reinforcements. Meanwhile the Continental army in the region grew stronger and more men were coming to join the fighting. A series of battles led to the defeat of the British at Saratoga, New York, in October 1777. Almost six thousand British troops surrendered.

② デラウェア川を横断するワシントン（トレントンの戦い）

　この戦争の重要な戦いの１つは、植民地人が真の勝利を収めたときでした。イギリスはドイツの兵士（ヘシアン）を雇い、植民地人と戦わせました。1776 年 12 月 25 日のクリスマスの夜、ヘシアンの軍隊はニュージャージー州のトレントンの町に陣を配置していました。寒い暗闇の中、ジョージ・ワシントン将軍とその軍隊は、凍りついたデラウェア川を渡って休んでいたヘシアン兵を攻撃し、その３分の２を殺害または捕虜にしました。この勝利はアメリカ植民地人を勇気づけました。

③ サラトガの戦い

　イギリスはカナダから数千の軍隊を植民地に送ってニューイングランドの州を占領し、植民地を半分に分断することを計画しました。イギリス軍はカナダを出発する際、十分な物資が供給されていました。一方、アメリカ兵は半ば飢えていて、服も装備も万全ではありませんでした。

　しかし、イギリス軍は南に移動するにつれ、アメリカ軍の攻撃によって予想よりも進行が遅れ、食糧、物資や援軍が不足し始めたのです。その間、この地域の植民地軍はさらに強くなり、より多くの人々がこの戦いに参加するために集まってきました。一連の戦いは、1777 年 10 月、ニューヨーク州のサラトガでイギリス軍が敗北したことで終了を迎えました。このとき、約 6,000 人のイギリス軍が降伏しました。

Vocabulary

- ☐ capture　捕獲する、捕らえる
- ☐ equipment　装備、備品
- ☐ meanwhile　そうしている間に
- ☐ encourage　勇気づける
- ☐ reinforcement　援軍、援兵
- ☐ surrender　降参する、降伏する

④ France Becomes an Ally

The victory at Saratoga was important because it brought America a strong ally: France. The French had secretly helped the Americans by sending supplies. But after the victory at Saratoga, the French openly supported the Americans by sending weapons and eventually troops. By June 1778, France and Britain were at war.

⑤ Valley Forge

British troops captured Philadelphia. In the bitter winter of 1777, they were warm and comfortable. Meanwhile, twenty miles northwest of the city, at Valley Forge, Washington and his troops were cold, hungry, and sick.

The winter at Valley Forge turned into the low point of the American Revolution. Many American soldiers died and others simply left and went home. General Washington did everything possible to encourage his troops to endure the harsh suffering of the winter that was part of the struggle for liberty.

④ フランスが同盟国に

　サラトガでの勝利は、アメリカにフランスという強力な同盟国ができたという点で重要でした。フランスは補給品を送ることで、以前は密かにアメリカ人を支援していました。しかしサラトガでの勝利の後、フランスは公然とアメリカ人を支援し、武器や、最終的には軍隊も送ったのです。1778 年 6 月には、フランスとイギリスは交戦状態になっていました。

⑤ バレーフォージ

　イギリス軍はフィラデルフィアを占領しました。1777 年の厳しい冬の間、彼ら（イギリス軍）は暖かく快適に過ごしていました。その一方で、フィラデルフィアから北西に 20 マイル（約 30 キロメートル）離れたバレーフォージで、ワシントン将軍と彼の軍隊は凍え、飢え、病んでいました。

　バレーフォージでの冬は、アメリカ独立戦争における最下点（最悪のとき）でした。多くのアメリカ兵が死亡し、故郷に帰ってしまう兵士たちもいました。ワシントン将軍は、冬の厳しい苦難も自由を勝ち取るための戦いの一部であると、苦しみに耐えるよう兵士たちを可能な限り励ましました。

Vocabulary

☐ ally　同盟国
☐ endure　耐える、耐え忍ぶ
☐ struggle　戦い

☐ bitter　厳しい
☐ harsh　厳しい

⑥ Battle of Yorktown and British Surrender

In an effort to conquer Virginia and defeat the Americans, British general Cornwallis marched his troops to Yorktown and prepared for battle. It was on a peninsula between the York and James rivers, which empty into Chesapeake Bay. It was an area that General Washington knew very well. It was a great advantage to the Americans.

Washington quickly marched south from New Jersey together with French soldiers under Lafayette. They surrounded the British on land, while the French navy prevented the British from escaping by sea.

Cornwallis's troops were forced to surrender in October, 1781. After a few more minor battles, the mighty British army was defeated. It was the end of the Revolutionary War.

⑥ ヨークタウンの戦いとイギリスの降伏

バージニアを征服してアメリカ軍を負かすために、イギリスのコーンウォリス将軍は軍隊をヨークタウンに進軍させ、戦闘の準備をしました。ヨークタウンは、チェサピーク湾に注ぎ込むヨーク川とジェームズ川の間にある半島にありました。ここはワシントン将軍がよく知っている地域だったので、それはアメリカ側に有利に働きました。

ワシントンは、ただちにニュージャージー州から南へ進軍しました。ラファイエットが率いるフランス兵も加わりました。彼らは陸上でイギリス軍を包囲し、フランス海軍はイギリス軍の海からの退路を遮りました。

1781 年 10 月、コーンウォリスの軍は降伏を余儀なくされました。その後、いくつかの小規模な戦いを経て、強力なイギリス軍は敗退し、独立戦争は終わったのです。

Vocabulary

□ conquer　征服する、打ち勝つ
□ advantage　有利な点
□ mighty　強力な、強大な
□ peninsula　半島
□ prevent　防ぐ

11 America Becomes Independent

A peace treaty signed in 1783 gave America the lands that reached from the Atlantic Ocean to the Mississippi River. The fighting was over. Now it was time for the Americans to create their own government.

The 13 Original States

New Hampshire

Massachusetts

Rhode Island

Connecticut

New York

New Jersey

Pennsylvania

Delaware

Maryland

Virginia

North Carolina

South Carolina

Georgia

Let's try it!

Q64 There were 13 original states. Name three.

→ Answer p.97

　1783 年に結ばれた平和条約により、アメリカは大西洋からミシシッピ川まで領土が広がりました。戦いは終わり、アメリカ人が独自の政府を作るときが来たのです。

13 の元植民地・独立 13 州

ニューハンプシャー州

マサチューセッツ州

ロードアイランド州

コネティカット州

ニューヨーク州

ニュージャージー州

ペンシルベニア州

デラウェア州

メリーランド州

バージニア州

ノースカロライナ州

サウスカロライナ州

ジョージア州

Vocabulary

☐ peace treaty　平和条約

12 Original 13 States

After the Americans won the Revolutionary War, they were no longer "colonies" under a faraway king. They were thirteen independent "states" and each wanted to be in charge of itself. None of them wanted a strong government telling them what to do.

Each wanted to make its own laws and have its own rulers. They couldn't even agree to use the same kind of money, so each state issued its own money.

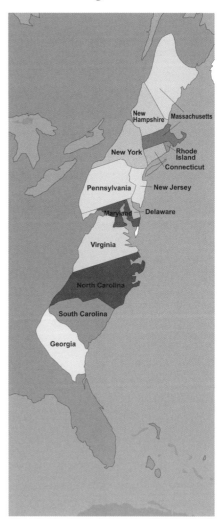

But they realized that on some occasions the thirteen states would have to join together as the United States of America. They would have to unite if England or another country attacked the United States. Someone would have to organize an American army, pay the soldiers, give orders, and watch out over all of the states together.

13の元植民地・独立13州

　アメリカ人は独立戦争に勝利し、アメリカはもう遠く離れた王の下にある「植民地」ではなくなりました。13の独立した「州」となり、それぞれが自治（自分たちで統治すること）を求めていました。どの州も強力な政府に命令されたくなかったのです。それぞれが自分たちの法律を作り、自分たちのリーダー（指導者）を持つことを望みました。彼らは統一の貨幣を使うことにすら同意できなかったので、各州はそれぞれの貨幣を発行しました。

　しかし、彼らは13の州がいつかはアメリカ合衆国としてまとまる必要があることに気がつきました。イギリスや他の国がアメリカを攻撃したとき、彼らは団結しなければなりません。誰かがアメリカ軍を組織し、兵士に給料を支払い、命令を下し、すべての州を共に統治しなければならないのです。

Vocabulary

☐ faraway　遠方の
☐ unite　団結する、結合する

☐ be in charge of　～を担当する

13 The Constitutional Convention

To discuss all of these issues, leaders from each state gathered at the Constitutional Convention. It was here that the leaders, referred to as "the Founding Fathers," debated issues and eventually produced the founding document of the country: the U. S. Constitution.

Although the Constitution was written in 1787, it did not go into effect automatically. First, it had to be approved by the voters of the thirteen original states. To explain why the Constitution was important and to encourage the people in each state to support its passage, several men wrote a series of 85 essays called the Federalist Papers. These essays were aimed at voters in New York State. However, they were highly influential in other states as well.

The Federalist Papers were written anonymously under the shared pen name Publius. They were actually written by Alexander Hamilton,

これらの課題を議論するため、各州から代表者（指導者）が憲法制定会議に集まりました。ここで、「アメリカ合衆国建国の父たち」と呼ばれるこの指導者たちは議論を重ね、後に建国文書である合衆国憲法を作ったのです。

憲法は1787年に書かれましたが、そのまま発効されたわけではありませんでした。まず、13の独立州の有権者によって承認されなければなりませんでした。憲法がなぜ重要であるかを説明し、各州の人々に成立を支持するよう促すため、数名の人物が"The Federalist Papers（『ザ・フェデラリスト』）"と呼ばれる85編の連作論文を執筆しました。これらの論文はニューヨーク州の有権者を対象としたものでしたが、他の州でも大きな影響力を発揮しました。

"The Federalist Papers"は、「パブリウス」という共通のペンネームが使用され匿名で書かれました。実際には、アレクサンダー・ハミルトン、ジェームズ・マディソン、そしてジョン・ジェイによって書かれたものです。これらの論文は、当時のアメリカが直面していた問題について論じるものとして重要でしたが、今日においても、政府はどのように機能すべきかを説明する意味で重要だとされて

James Madison. Notes for Speech on Constitutional Amendments.

James Madison, and John Jay. These essays were important as discussions of the problems America faced then and even today they are considered valuable explanations of how government should function.

The first page of the U.S. Constitution begins with "We the People." The Constitution is not a law created by a king or an emperor, who is all-powerful and tells everyone what they must do. It is "the American people" who themselves choose this new kind of government.

Let's try it!

Q 65   What happened at the Constitutional Convention?

Q 66   When was the Constitution written?

Q 67   The Federalist Papers supported the passage of the U.S. Constitution. Name one of the writers.

→ Answer p.97

います。

　アメリカ合衆国憲法の最初のページは"We the People（われら国民は）"
という言葉で始まっています。憲法は、絶対的な権力を持ち、すべての人々に
命令を下す王や皇帝が作った法律ではありません。「われら（合衆国の）人民」、
つまりすべてのアメリカ人自身がこの新しい形の政府を選んだのです。

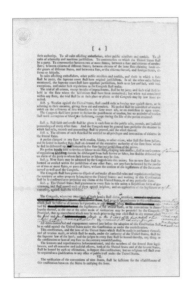

George Washington Papers,
Constitution, Printed, with Marginal Notes by George Washington

Vocabulary

☐ convention　集会、協議会
☐ federalist　連邦主義者
☐ function　機能する

☐ founding　創設の
☐ be aimed at　〜を目標にする

89

14 Major Figures of Early America

① Benjamin Franklin

Benjamin Franklin was famous for many different achievements. Franklin was a publisher, an inventor, scientist, entrepreneur, politician, and the first Postmaster General of the United States. He established the first public library in America, in a time when books were expensive and not available to the public. He published an annual almanac called *Poor Richard's Almanack* and included in it many sayings that are well known today such as: "Time is money." "Early to bed and early to rise, makes a man healthy, wealthy, and wise." "A penny saved is a penny earned."

He was the oldest member of the Constitutional Convention and was well respected. As an American diplomat, he served as Ambassador to France, from 1776 to 1785.

 *Let's try it!*

Q68 What is one thing Benjamin Franklin is famous for?

→ Answer p.97

初期アメリカの代表的人物

① ベンジャミン・フランクリン

ベンジャミン・フランクリンは様々な功績を残したことで有名です。フランクリンは出版業者、発明家、科学者、実業家、政治家であり、アメリカの初代郵便局長でした。書籍が高価で一般では手に入れられない時代のアメリカで、初の公立図書館を設立しました。彼は毎年、

『プーア・リチャードの暦（Poor Richard's Almanack）』という暦を発行し、その中には「時は金なり」「早寝早起きは、人を健康、富裕、賢明にする」「1銭（1ペニー）の節約は1銭（1ペニー）の儲け（塵も積もれば山となる）」など、今もよく知られている格言が数多く含まれています。

彼は憲法制定会議の最年長メンバーであり、とても尊敬されていました。また、アメリカの外交官として、1776年から1785年まで在フランスのアメリカ大使を務めました。

Vocabulary

- ☐ entrepreneur　実業家
- ☐ almanac　暦書
- ☐ wealthy　裕福な
- ☐ Postmaster General　郵便局長
- ☐ sayings　格言、ことわざ
- ☐ diplomat　外交官

② George Washington

George Washington was the General of
the Colonial Army during the Revolutionary
War. Because he was widely respected, he
became the leader of the Constitutional
Convention in Philadelphia in 1787.
Representatives from the original thirteen

states discussed and wrote the Constitution. Washington became
the first President of the United States in 1789. He served two
terms—declining a third term—before retiring. He is respectfully
and gratefully referred to as the "Father of Our Country" for his
leadership during its early years.

③ Thomas Jefferson

Thomas Jefferson was one of the most important of the Founding
Fathers of the country. He was the main author of the Declaration
of Independence, served as the first Secretary of State, and served
as the third President. During his presidency, he concluded the
Louisiana Purchase in 1803. This land west of the Mississippi
River, purchased from France, more than doubled the size of
American territory. He is also famed as a champion of political and
religious freedom.

⸞ Let's try it!

Q69 Who is the "Father of Our Country"?
Q70 Who was the first President?

→ Answer p.97

② ジョージ・ワシントン

　ジョージ・ワシントンは独立戦争中の植民地軍の将軍（総司令官）でした。人々から広く尊敬されていたため、1787 年にフィラデルフィアで開かれた憲法制定会議の議長に選出されました。ここでは独立 13 州の代表者が議論し、憲法の文書を作りました。そして 1789 年、ワシントンは初代のアメリカ合衆国大統領に就任しました。2 期の任期を務めた後、（3 期目を拒否して）退任しました。建国初期の、彼のリーダーシップへの敬意と称賛を込めて「建国の父」と呼ばれています。

③ トーマス・ジェファーソン

　トーマス・ジェファーソンは、アメリカ合衆国建国の父の中で最も重要な人物の 1 人です。彼は独立宣言の主要な執筆者であり、初代国務長官、そして第 3 代大統領を務めました。大統領在任中の 1803 年、彼はルイジアナ買収を成立させました。ミシシッピ川の西のこの土地をフランスから購入したことで、アメリカの領土を倍以上に拡大させたのです。また、彼は政治的・宗教的自由の擁護者としても有名です。

Vocabulary

- ☐ term　期
- ☐ be referred to　〜と言われている
- ☐ double　2 倍に
- ☐ respectfully　敬意を表して
- ☐ author　執筆者、創造者
- ☐ champion　（主張の）擁護者

④ James Madison

James Madison worked hard to find a way for the states to work together and settle disagreements. The states agreed that they needed a leader to run the country, but they did not want a powerful king, so they decided on having a president, who was not too powerful.  They agreed that the states would work together to make the laws for the whole country and called the lawmakers Congress.

When disagreements about the law arose, they would have a court system—with the Supreme Court at the top—decide how to settle the issues. All of these ideas were put together in the highest law of the country: the United States Constitution. James Madison worked hard to get the Constitution written and many of his ideas are in it, and so he is known as "the Father of the Constitution."

⑤ Alexander Hamilton

Alexander Hamilton, another Founding Father of the United States, was an aide to General George Washington during the Revolutionary War. Hamilton wrote many of the Federalist Papers and was a leader in the writing of the draft of the United States Constitution. He helped establish the First Bank of the United States and was the first Secretary of the Treasury. He was politically opposed by Thomas Jefferson.

④ ジェームズ・マディソン

　ジェームズ・マディソンは、各州が協力し合い、意見の不一致を解決する方法を探るために努力しました。州は国を運営する指導者が必要であることには同意しましたが、強力な王を置くことは望まなかったので、そこまで大きな権力を持たない大統領を置くことにしたのです。彼らは、州が協力して国全体の法律を作ることに合意し、法律を作る人たちのことを議会と呼びました。

　法律について意見の不一致が生じた場合、最高裁判所が監督する裁判制度によって解決方法を決めることにしました。これらの考え方はすべて国の最高法規である合衆国憲法に集約されました。ジェームズ・マディソンは、憲法制定に向けて力を尽くし、彼のアイディアの多くが憲法に盛り込まれていることから、彼は「合衆国憲法の父」として知られています。

⑤ アレクサンダー・ハミルトン

　もう1人のアメリカ合衆国建国の父であるアレクサンダー・ハミルトンは、独立戦争中のジョージ・ワシントン将軍の副官でした。ハミルトンは"The Federalist Papers"の多くの部分を執筆し、合衆国憲法の草稿作成のリーダーでした。アメリカの第一合衆国銀行の設立に貢献し、初代財務長官でもありました。しかし政治的にはトーマス・ジェファーソンと対立していました。

Vocabulary

☐ settle　解決する、処理する　　☐ disagreement　意見の相違
☐ lawmaker　立法者（の団体）　　☐ Treasury　財務省

Let's Try Test Questions

Page 82

Q 64 There were 13 original states. Name three.

Page 88

Q 65 What happened at the Constitutional Convention?

Q 66 When was the Constitution written?

Q 67 The Federalist Papers supported the passage of the U.S. Constitution. Name one of the writers.

Page 90

Q 68 What is one thing Benjamin Franklin is famous for?

Page 92

Q 69 Who is the "Father of Our Country"?

Q 70 Who was the first President?

Answers

A 64 独立した当初は 13 の州がありました。そのうち 3 州を挙げてください。
New Hampshire ニューハンプシャー州，**Massachusetts** マサチューセッツ州，**Rhode Island** ロードアイランド州，**Connecticut** コネティカット州，**New York** ニューヨーク州，**New Jersey** ニュージャージー州，**Pennsylvania** ペンシルベニア州，**Delaware** デラウェア州，**Maryland** メリーランド州，**Virginia** バージニア州，**North Carolina** ノースカロライナ州，**South Carolina** サウスカロライナ州，**Georgia** ジョージア州

A 65 憲法制定会議では何が起きましたか？
The Constitution was written. 憲法が書かれた，**The Founding Fathers wrote the Constitution.** ファウンディング・ファーザーズ（建国の父たち）が憲法を書いた

A 66 憲法が書かれたのはいつですか？
1787 1787 年

A 67 『ザ・フェデラリスト』はアメリカ合衆国憲法の成立を支援しました。その執筆者を 1 人挙げてください。
(James) Madison（ジェームズ）マディソン，**(Alexander) Hamilton**（アレクサンダー）ハミルトン，**(John) Jay**（ジョン）ジェイ，**Publius** パブリウス

A 68 ベンジャミン・フランクリンはどのようなことで有名ですか？ その 1 つを挙げてください。
U.S. diplomat アメリカ合衆国の外交官，**Oldest member of the Constitutional Convention** 憲法制定会議の最年長委員，**First Postmaster General of the United States** アメリカ合衆国初の郵便局長，**Writer of "Poor Richard's Almanack"** 『プーア・リチャードの暦』の作者，**Started the first free libraries** 初の無料公共図書館を設立した

A 69 「建国の父」は誰ですか？
(George) Washington（ジョージ）ワシントン

A 70 初代アメリカ合衆国大統領は誰ですか？
(George) Washington（ジョージ）ワシントン

15 The Louisiana Purchase and Two Wars

In 1803 President Thomas Jefferson ordered negotiations with France over the huge Louisiana Territory. The area extended between the Mississippi River and the Rocky Mountains. The Louisiana Purchase more than doubled the size of the United States.

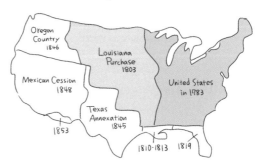

① The War of 1812

The War of 1812 fought between Britain and the United States lasted from 1812 to 1815. As a result of this background, it has been called the second American war for independence. It began over disagreements regarding shipping rights. American soldiers attacked Canada, a British colony, unsuccessfully and the British retaliated by burning the White House and other buildings in Washington, D.C. The greatest American victory came in the Battle of New Orleans. Ironically, a peace treaty was signed before that battle, but the armies were not informed in time. Despite the fact that a cease-fire had been agreed upon, this battle caused a large number of casualties.

ルイジアナ買収と 2 つの戦争

　1803 年、トーマス・ジェファーソン大統領はルイジアナ領土についてフランスと交渉するよう命じました。この土地はミシシッピ川からロッキー山脈まで広がっていました。このルイジアナ買収はアメリカの領土を 2 倍以上に拡大させました。

Napoleon Signing Cession of Louisiana.

① 1812 年の戦争（米英戦争）

　アメリカとイギリスが戦った 1812 年の戦争は 1812 年から 1815 年まで続きました。その背景から「第二次アメリカ独立戦争」とも呼ばれました。発端は、商船の往来に関する対立でした。アメリカはイギリスの領土となっていたカナダを攻撃しましたが失敗し、イギリスは報復のために、ワシントン D.C. のホワイトハウスや他の建物に火を放ったのです。アメリカは、ニューオーリンズでの戦いで最大の勝利を迎えました。皮肉なことに、その戦いの前に平和条約（ガン条約という講和条約）が結ばれましたが、その知らせが届くのには時間がかかり軍には伝わっていなかったのです。正式に停戦が決まったにもかかわらず、この戦いで多くの犠牲者が出てしまいました。

② The Mexican-American War

The Mexican-American War was fought between 1846 and 1848. The American government was encouraged by the feelings of many Americans that the country had a "manifest destiny" to expand westward.

As a result of the war, America claimed land north of the Rio Grande River in Texas and territory that includes the current states of California, Nevada, and Utah, and parts of other states.

 Let's try it!

Q71 What territory did the United States buy from France in 1803?

→ Answer p.127

② アメリカ・メキシコ戦争（米墨戦争）

アメリカ・メキシコ戦争は 1846 年から 1848 年まで続きました。アメリカ政府は、西部へ領土を拡大することは"manifest destiny（明白な運命）"だという、多くのアメリカ人が抱いていた思想に後押しされたのです。

戦争の結果、アメリカはテキサス州にあるリオグランデ川の北にある、現在のカリフォルニア州、ネバダ州、ユタ州、そして他の州の部分を含む土地に国土を広げました。

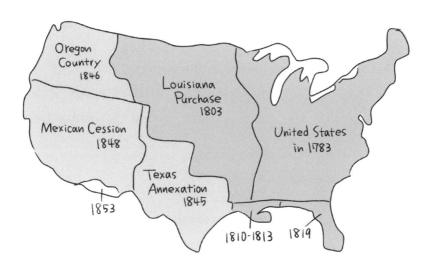

Vocabulary

- [ ] negotiation 交渉
- [ ] cease-fire 停戦
- [ ] ironically 皮肉にも、意外と
- [ ] casualties 死傷者

16 The Civil War (1861-1865)

The Civil War was a war between the states of the North and the states of the South. The two sides had different views of several issues. Eventually the disagreements became so strong that the country split into two parts. The Northern states were called "the Union." The Southern states were called "the Confederacy." Let's look at the problems that led to the split.

Let's try it!

Q73 Name the U.S. war between the North and the South.

→ Answer p.127

南北戦争

　南北戦争は北部と南部の州の間での戦争（内戦）でした。両者の意見の相違が深刻になり、後に国が2つに分断されてしまったのです。北部は"Union"、南部は"Confederacy"と呼ばれました。北部と南部が分裂に至った原因を見ていきましょう。

Vocabulary

☐ issue　課題、問題
☐ confederacy　同盟、連合（Confederacy ＝ 南部）
☐ union　同盟、連合（Union ＝ 北部）

17 Causes of the Civil War

① Slavery

One problem was slavery. People from Africa were captured and sold to slave traders, who sold those people in America. Slaves had no rights and no freedom. The laws of America did not protect them, because they were not considered American citizens. Slave owners treated them cruelly and bought and sold them like property. The Northern states wanted to end slavery for several reasons. One reason was because it was a cruel system. Because the Southern states said that they needed slaves to do the work of farms and large plantations, they wanted to maintain the system of slavery. They did not want the North to tell them how their society should function.

In Congress, slavery caused problems in the balance of power between the North and the South. When America was formed, it was important to get the North and the South to agree on how many Senators and Representatives to send to Congress. As a compromise, slaves were counted as "3/5ths of a (white) person." That did not mean slaves had any rights. It did mean that the South had a large population, so the South had significant influence in politics. In fact, many of the early Presidents and members of Congress were slave-owners from the South, including George Washington and Thomas Jefferson.

南北戦争を引き起こした原因

① 奴隷制度

　1つ目の問題は、奴隷制度（をめぐる意見の相違）でした。アフリカから来た人々は捕らえられて奴隷商人に売られ、奴隷商人たちは彼らをアメリカで売りました。奴隷には権利も自由もありませんでした。アメリカの国民としてみなされなかったため、法律は彼らを守ってくれませんでした。奴隷所有者は彼らを残酷に扱い、所有物のように売買しました。北部の州はいくつかの理由で奴隷制度を終わらせたいと考えました。1つは、道徳的に問題のある制度だからです。南部の州は、農場やプランテーションでの労働力として依存していたため、奴隷制度を維持しようとしました。北部に社会がどのように機能するべきかと口出ししてほしくなかったのです。

　議会では、奴隷制度は北部と南部の間のパワーバランスに問題を引き起こしていました。アメリカの建国時、北部と南部が何名の上院・下院議員を議会に送るかについて合意することが重要でした。そこで妥協案として、奴隷は「（白人）1人に対して5分の3人」として数えることで合意しました。しかしそれは、奴隷に権利があったことを意味するわけではありません。南部は人口が多かったため、政治に大きな影響力を持つことを意味しました。実際には、ジョージ・ワシントンやトーマス・ジェファーソンを含む初期の大統領や議員の多くも南部の奴隷所有者でした。

Vocabulary

- [ ] citizen　市民、国民
- [ ] Senator　（米）上院議員
- [ ] property　所有物、財産
- [ ] Representative　（米）下院議員

② Economy

A second reason was economic. There were major differences between the economies of the North and the South. While the South was dependent on agriculture and slave labor, in the North industry was progressing, with factories producing steel and machinery. People in the United States had to pay taxes to buy and sell products overseas. The North had lots of factories and taxes helped protect these factories from overseas competition. This prevented Britain and other European countries from selling cheaper goods in America. In the South, however, taxes made their farm products more expensive overseas. Southern farm and plantation owners wanted freedom from taxes.

② 経済

　2つ目は経済的理由でした。北部と南部では経済が大きく異なりました。南部は農業と奴隷の労働力に頼っていましたが、北部は鉄鋼や機械などを生産する工場が基盤となり、工業化が進んでいたのです。また、アメリカ合衆国の人々は海外で商品を売買する際、関税が課せられていました。北部にはたくさんの工場があり、関税はその工場を海外の競争から守っていました。イギリスをはじめ他のヨーロッパの国々がより安価な商品をアメリカで販売するのを防いでいたのです。しかし、南部ではその関税によって農産物が海外では高額になりました。南部の農場やプランテーションの所有者は関税から解放されたいと考えていました。

③ States' Rights

A third reason concerned what is called "states' rights." You will remember that the federal government has certain rights and duties and the state governments have other rights and duties. The North believed that federal laws should be more powerful than state laws. The South believed that state laws should be stronger, because local people were better at making decisions about local problems.

The combination of these disagreements led to the division of the young country into two basic parts: the Union (the Northern states) and the Confederacy (the Southern states). Between 1860 and 1861 eleven southern states left the Union and became the Confederate States of America. And in 1861 the Civil War began.

Let's try it! ───────────────────────────

Q74 **Name one problem that led to the Civil War.**

→ Answer p.127

③ 州の権限

3つ目は「州の権限」と呼ばれる概念でした。連邦政府には特定の権限や務めがあり、州政府にもその他の権限や務めがあることを覚えているでしょう。北部は、連邦法は州法より優位であると主張していました。反対に、南部は、その地域の人々のほうが現地の問題についてより良い決断ができるということから、州法のほうが優位であると主張しました。

これらの対立が合わさり、この若い国が"Union（合衆国北部の州）"と"Confederacy（南部連合軍、南部の州）"に2分される原因となったのです。1860年から1861年の間に11の南部の州が合衆国を離脱し、南部連合に加わりました。そして、1861年に南北戦争が勃発したのです。

Vocabulary

☐ overseas　海外に（の）　　☐ states' rights　州の権限
☐ duty　義務　　☐ lead to　〜につながる

18 The Underground Railway

Before and during the Civil War, secret groups of people opposed to slavery participated in an organization known as the Underground Railway. Of course, it was not a railway and it was not underground. It was a network of people who cooperated to assist slaves in escaping from their masters in the South in order to reach safe places in the North and in Canada. Their activities were dangerous, so they operated at night. Safe houses where escaping slaves could stay were known as "stations," and people who guided them to safety were known as "conductors."

Born into slavery, Harriet Tubman escaped to the North by the Underground Railway in 1849. Despite the danger of being caught, she made frequent (19 or more) secret trips into the South to lead over 300 slaves to freedom. Known as the "Moses of her people," she was admired by abolitionists. During the Civil War, she served as a

nurse, scout, and a spy for the Northern army in the South.

「地下鉄道」

　南北戦争以前とその真っ只中でも、奴隷制度に反対する人々は「地下鉄道」と呼ばれる組織に参加しました。もちろん、実際には鉄道ではなく、地下でもありません。それは、南部の奴隷たちを主人の元から逃亡させ、北部やカナダの安全な場所へ誘導するのを手伝った人たちでした。その活動は危険だったため、夜に行われました。逃亡中の隠れ家となる家は「駅」として知られ、安全な場所に誘導する人は「車掌」と呼ばれました。

　ハリエット・タブマンは奴隷として生まれ、1849 年に「地下鉄道」を通して北部へ逃れました。捕われる危険がありながらも、彼女は頻繁に（19 回以上）南部に潜入し、300 人以上の奴隷の逃亡を助けたのです。彼女は「黒いモーゼ」と呼ばれ、奴隷廃止論者に慕われました。南北戦争中、彼女は看護師、そして南部では偵察者、北軍のスパイとして活動しました。

Vocabulary

☐ cooperate　協力する

☐ Moses　モーゼ

☐ master　（奴隷の）主人

☐ abolitionist　（奴隷制度）廃止論者

19 Events and Ending of the Civil War

The first battle of the war was at Fort Sumter, in the harbor of Charleston, South Carolina. This happened shortly after Abraham Lincoln of the Republican Party was elected President.

Among the major battles of war was the Battle of Vicksburg. Union troops defeated the Confederate troops and gained control of the Mississippi River there in 1863.

Also in 1863, the Battle of Gettysburg in Pennsylvania was followed by the dedication of the Gettysburg National Cemetery. On that occasion, President Lincoln delivered the speech called the Gettysburg Address. His speech called everyone gathered that day to dedicate themselves to work together so that "government of the people, by the people, for the people, shall not perish from the earth."

While the Civil War was continuing, on January 1, 1863, President Lincoln issued the Emancipation Proclamation. "Emancipation" means that a person gains freedom. It did not free all of the slaves. It only freed slaves in the South, in those states that had left the Union. But it was the first step toward ending slavery in the United States. Later the Thirteenth Amendment to the Constitution would permanently end slavery everywhere in the country.

南北戦争の出来事と終結

戦争はサウスカロライナ州チャールストン湾内にあるサムター要塞から始まりました。それは共和党のエイブラハム・リンカーンが大統領に当選したすぐ後でした。

そのなかでの主な戦闘はヴィックスバーグでの戦いでした。1863 年、北軍はここで南軍を制圧し、ミシシッピ川を支配下に収めました。

同じく 1863 年、ペンシルベニア州でのゲティスバーグの戦いの後に、ゲティスバーグの国立墓地で戦没者に向けた奉献式がありました。そこで、リンカーン大統領は「ゲティスバーグの演説」と呼ばれるスピーチを行いました。(アメリカ史上最も有名な演説の 1 つとなったこの演説で)彼はすべてのアメリカ人が「人民の、人民による、人民のための政治を、この地上から消え失せないように」するために共に力を合わせて献身するよう呼びかけたのです。

南北戦争が続く中、1863 年 1 月 1 日にリンカーン大統領は奴隷解放宣言を公表しました。"Emancipation(解放)"は自由の身とすることを意味しますが、すべての奴隷が自由になったわけではありませんでした。連邦を離脱した、南部連合の支配する地域の奴隷のみが対象でした。それでもこれは、アメリカで奴隷制度を終わらせる最初の一歩でした。その後、憲法修正第 13 条により、全米のあらゆる場所で奴隷制度が永久に廃止されることになりました。

End of the Civil War

On April 9, 1865, General Robert E. Lee of the Confederacy surrendered to Union General Ulysses S. Grant. The victory of the Northern army ended the Civil War. Differences between the North and the South remained, but the fighting was over.

The Gettysburg Address (November 19, 1863)

Four score and seven years ago our fathers brought forth on this continent, a new nation, conceived in Liberty, and dedicated to the proposition that all men are created equal.

Now we are engaged in a great civil war, testing whether that nation, or any nation so conceived and so dedicated, can long endure. We are met on a great battle-field of that war. We have come to dedicate a portion of that field, as a final resting place for those who here gave their lives that that nation might live. It is altogether fitting and proper that we should do this.

But, in a larger sense, we can not dedicate – we can not consecrate – we can not hallow – this ground. The brave men, living and dead, who struggled here, have consecrated it, far above our poor power to add or detract. The world will little note, nor long remember what we say here, but it can never forget what they did here. It is for us the living, rather, to be dedicated here to the unfinished work which they who fought here have thus far so nobly advanced. It is rather for us to be here dedicated to the great task remaining before us – that from these honored dead we take increased devotion to that cause for which they gave the last full measure of devotion – that we here highly resolve that these dead shall not have died in vain – that this nation, under God, shall have a new birth of freedom—and that government of the people, by the people, for the people, shall not perish from the earth.

Let's try it!

Q76 **What did the Emancipation Proclamation do?**

→ Answer p.127

南北戦争の終結

　1865 年 4 月 9 日、南部連合軍の司令官、ロバート・E・リー将軍が、北軍（連邦軍）の司令官、ユリシーズ・S・グラント将軍に降伏し、北軍の勝利で南北戦争は終結しました。北部と南部の間で違いは残りましたが、戦いは終わったのです。

ゲティスバーグの演説（1863 年 11 月 19 日）

87 年前、われわれの父祖たちは、自由の精神にはぐくまれ、人はみな平等に創られているという信条にささげられた新しい国家を、この大陸に誕生させた。

今われわれは、一大内戦のさなかにあり、戦うことにより、自由の精神をはぐくみ、自由の心情にささげられたこの国家が、或いは、このようなあらゆる国家が、長く存続することは可能なのかどうかを試しているわけである。われわれはそのような戦争に一大激戦の地で、相会している。われわれはこの国家が生き永らえるようにと、ここで生命を捧げた人々の最後の安息の場所として、この戦場の一部をささげるためにやって来た。われわれがそうすることは、まことに適切であり好ましいことである。

しかし、さらに大きな意味で、われわれは、この土地をささげることはできない。清めささげることもできない。聖別することもできない。足すことも引くこともできない、われわれの貧弱な力をはるかに超越し、生き残った者、戦死した者とを問わず、ここで闘った勇敢な人々がすでに、この土地を清めささげているからである。世界は、われわれがここで述べることに、さして注意を払わず、長く記憶にとどめることもないだろう。しかし、彼らがここで成した事を決して忘れ去ることはできない。ここで戦った人々が気高くもここまで勇敢に推し進めてきた未完の事業にここでささげるべきは、むしろ生きているわれわれなのである。われわれの目の前に残された偉大な事業にここで身をささげるべきは、むしろわれわれ自身なのである。―それは、名誉ある戦死者たちが、最後の全力を尽くして身命をささげた偉大な大義に対して、彼らの後を受け継いで、われわれが一層の献身を決意することであり、これらの戦死者の死を決して無駄にしないために、この国に神の下で自由の新しい誕生を迎えさせるために、そして、人民の人民による人民のための政治を地上から決して絶滅させないために、われわれがここで固く決意することである。

Vocabulary

☐ cemetery　墓地

☐ emancipation　（奴隷）解放

☐ perish　絶滅する、なくなる

☐ proclamation　宣言

20 Abraham Lincoln

Abraham Lincoln became the sixteenth president in March 1861 and he led the United States during the Civil War. As the leader of the Northern states, he wanted to save the Union. That is, he wanted to keep the Northern and Southern states together, not divided.

He signed the Emancipation Proclamation in 1863. It freed slaves in all of the Southern states.

Tragically, five days after the Civil War ended, President Lincoln was assassinated. Vice President Andrew Johnson became the next President.

☀ *Let's try it!*

Q75 **What was one important thing that Abraham Lincoln did?**

→ Answer p.127

エイブラハム・リンカーン

　エイブラハム・リンカーンは 1861 年 3 月に 16 代目大統領として就任し、南北戦争中のアメリカを率いました。北部の州のリーダーとして連邦を救いたい、つまり北部と南部の州を分断せず一緒にしておきたかったのです。

　彼は 1863 年、奴隷解放宣言に署名し、南部の州のすべての奴隷を自由にしました。

　悲劇的なことに、南北戦争終結の 5 日後にリンカーン大統領は暗殺されました。アンドリュー・ジョンソン副大統領が大統領の後継者となりました。

Abraham Lincoln papers
(Gettysburg Address: Nicolay Copy)

21 Reconstruction (1865-1877) and Constitutional Amendments

Following the end of the Civil War, the President and the Congress of the United States set policy standards for the return of the Southern states. These states had to meet the standards in order to rejoin the United States officially. In addition, the Congress passed three important amendments to the Constitution.

Three Constitutional Amendments

The Thirteenth Amendment ended slavery and other kinds of involuntary servitude.

The Fourteenth Amendment granted civil rights and equal protection under the law to people who had formerly been enslaved. This made all Blacks citizens of the United States.

The Fifteenth Amendment granted voting rights to formerly enslaved men. This meant that all men—Black and white—could vote. But women—Black and white—did not have the right to vote yet.

南部再建と憲法修正

　南北戦争が終わると、大統領と合衆国議会は南部連合の州を合衆国に復帰させるための政策基準を設定しました。これらの州は、その基準を満たさないと合衆国に正式に復帰できませんでした。さらに、議会は3つの重要な憲法修正を可決しました。

3つの憲法修正

　憲法修正第13条は、奴隷制度および本人の意に反するその他の苦役を廃止しました。

　憲法修正第14条は、奴隷から解放された人々に対し、市民権と、法の下で平等に保護される権利を与えました。これにより、すべての黒人はアメリカ合衆国の市民となりました。

　憲法修正第15条は、奴隷から解放された男性に投票権を認めました。つまり、黒人も白人も、すべての男性は投票できるようになったのです。しかし女性については、黒人であっても白人であっても、まだ投票権はありませんでした。

Vocabulary

- [ ] reconstruction　再建
- [ ] policy　政策
- [ ] involuntary　不本意な
- [ ] amendment　修正
- [ ] rejoin　再び参加する
- [ ] servitude　奴隷状態、隷属

22 The Spanish-American War

This war between Spain and the United States was fought in 1898. It began with the explosion of the United States battleship *Maine* in the harbor of Havana, Cuba. The United States won the war with few casualties in a short period of time. As a result, the United States acquired Puerto Rico, Guam, and the Philippines. It gained temporary control over Cuba.

This war made the United States a world power, with territories stretching from the Caribbean Sea across the Pacific Ocean. Hawaii, which had been an independent kingdom, was annexed by the United States during this same period.

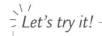
Let's try it!

Q72) Name one war fought by the United States in the 1800s.

→ Answer p.127

アメリカ・スペイン戦争（米西戦争）

　1898年、スペインとアメリカの間でこの戦争が起きました。発端は、キューバのハバナ港におけるアメリカ軍艦メイン号の爆沈でした。アメリカは犠牲が少なく短期間で勝利をおさめました。結果、アメリカはプエルトリコ、グアム、そしてフィリピンを獲得しました。また、一時的にキューバを支配下におきました。

　この戦争によってアメリカは、カリブ海から太平洋にまたがる領土を持つ世界の大国となりました。独立王国であったハワイも、この時期にアメリカに併合されました。

Vocabulary

☐ explosion　爆発
☐ casualties　死傷者
☐ annex　併合する

☐ battleship　軍艦
☐ acquire　獲得する

121

23 Women's Rights Movement in the 1800s

In the 1800s women had few rights. They could not vote, attend most colleges, or own property. In 1848 in Seneca Falls, New York, Susan B. Anthony, Elizabeth Cady Stanton, and other courageous women and men gathered to demand equality for women. Anthony and Stanton helped form the National Woman Suffrage Association. "Suffrage" means the right to vote. They gave speeches and organized petitions to gather support for an amendment to the U.S. Constitution to give women the right to vote.

Many politicians and citizens opposed this movement, but finally, in 1920, the Nineteenth Amendment was added to the Constitution, saying "The rights of citizens of the United States to vote shall not be denied or abridged by the United States or by any State on account of sex." This gave women the right to vote.

Let's try it!

Q77 **What did Susan B. Anthony do?**

→ Answer p.127

1880年代の女性権利運動（女権運動）

　1880年代、女性には限られた権利しかありませんでした。投票することも、ほとんどの大学に通うことも、土地を保有することもできませんでした。1848年、ニューヨークのセネカフォールズで、スーザン・B・アンソニー、エリザベス・キャディ・スタントン、そしてその他の勇気ある女性と男性が集まり、女性の平等の権利を訴えました。アンソニーとスタントンは"National Woman Suffrage Association（全米女性参政権協会）"の立ち上げに貢献しました。"Suffrage"は「参政権」を意味します。スピーチや請願活動を通して、女性に投票権を与えるアメリカ合衆国憲法の修正案に支持を集めました。

　多くの政治家や市民がこの運動に反対しましたが、1920年、ついに合衆国憲法修正第19条が憲法に追加され、「アメリカ合衆国市民の投票権は、合衆国またはいかなる州によっても、性別を理由に拒否または制限されてはいけない」とされました。これにより、女性に投票する権利が与えられたのです。

Elizabeth Cady Stanton, seated,
and Susan B. Anthony, standing on the right

Vocabulary

- [ ] attend　参加する、通う
- [ ] suffrage　参政権、選挙権
- [ ] deny　否定する
- [ ] demand　要求する
- [ ] petition　請願書
- [ ] abridge　（権利を）奪う

24 Sojourner Truth

Sojourner Truth was an African-American woman born into slavery in New York in 1795. She gained her freedom when New York state freed its slaves. Giving up her given name, she began calling herself Sojourner Truth, because she saw herself as "traveling from place to place helping people see the truth." She never learned to read and write, but she spoke powerfully in support of the abolition of slavery and women's rights. Her activism was aimed at helping America live up to its ideas of justice and equality.

In commemoration of the 200th anniversary of the birth of Sojourner Truth, NASA's Jet Propulsion Laboratory announced that it had chosen the name "Sojourner" for its Mars Planetary Rover.

ソジャーナ・トゥルース

　ソジャーナ・トゥルースは 1795 年、ニューヨークで奴隷の家族に生まれたアフリカ系アメリカ人の女性です。ニューヨーク州が奴隷を解放した際に自由を獲得しました。彼女は与えられた名前を捨て、自らをソジャーナ・トゥルース（「旅行者／滞在者・真実」の意味）と名乗り始めました。自身が「様々な場所を旅して、人に真実を見せる手助けをしている」と感じたからです。彼女は読み書きを学んだことはありませんでしたが、奴隷廃止と女性の権利を力強く訴えました。彼女の活動の背景には、アメリカが正義と平等という理念を実現するための手助けをする目的がありました。

　ソジャーナ・トゥルースの生誕 200 周年を記念して、NASA のジェット推進研究所は、火星探査機の名前を「ソジャーナ」とすることを発表しました。

Vocabulary

□ given name　与えられた名前　　□ activism　活動

Let's Try Test Questions

Q 71 What territory did the United States buy from France in 1803?

Q 73 Name the U.S. war between the North and the South.

Q 74 Name one problem that led to the Civil War.

Q 76 What did the Emancipation Proclamation do?

Q 75 What was one important thing that Abraham Lincoln did?

Q 72 Name one war fought by the United States in the 1800s.

Q 77 What did Susan B. Anthony do?

Answers

A71 アメリカ合衆国が 1803 年にフランスから購入した領土はどこですか？
Louisiana Territory ルイジアナ領土, **Louisiana** ルイジアナ州

A73 アメリカの北（北軍）と南（南軍）が戦った戦争の名前を挙げてください。
The Civil War 南北戦争, **The War between the States** 諸州間の戦争（北部と南部の間の内戦）

A74 南北戦争を引き起こした問題を 1 つ挙げてください。
Slavery 奴隷制度, **Economic reasons** 経済的な理由, **States' rights** 州の権利

A76 奴隷解放宣言は何をしましたか？
Freed the slaves 奴隷を解放した, **Freed slaves in the Confederacy** 南部連合の奴隷を解放した, **Freed slaves in the Confederate states** アメリカ連合国（南部連合国）の奴隷を解放した, **Freed slaves in most Southern states** 南部のほとんどの州の奴隷を解放した

A75 エイブラハム・リンカーンが行った重要なことの 1 つを挙げてください。
Freed the slaves (Emancipation Proclamation) 奴隷を解放した（奴隷解放宣言）, **Saved (or preserved) the Union** ユニオン（連邦）を守った, **Led the United States during the Civil War** 南北戦争中に（アメリカ合衆国大統領として）指揮にあたった

A72 アメリカが 1800 年代に戦った戦争を 1 つ挙げてください。
War of 1812 1812 年の戦争、米英戦争, **Mexican-American War** アメリカ・メキシコ戦争、米墨戦争, **Civil War** 南北戦争, **Spanish-American War** アメリカ・スペイン戦争、米西戦争

A77 スーザン・B・アンソニーは何をした人物ですか？
Fought for women's rights 女性の権利のために闘った, **Fought for civil rights** 公民権のために闘った

25 World War I (1914-1918)

In 1914 war broke out in Europe. It involved so many nations that it was called the Great War, or the World War. Later, after World War II, it came to be called the First World War or World War I.

On one side were the Allies, led by France and Britain. On the other side were the Central Powers, led by Germany.

Most Americans sympathized with France and Britain, but they were grateful to be living in a peaceful country, separated from the fighting by the Atlantic Ocean. They agreed with the decision of the United States government to remain neutral, that is, not to take a side in the fighting. But several events made Americans angry enough to enter the conflict.

第一次世界大戦

　1914 年、ヨーロッパで戦争が勃発しました。たくさんの国々を巻き込んだため、世界大戦と呼ばれました。第二次世界大戦以降は、第一次世界大戦と呼ばれるようになりました。

　一方にはフランスとイギリスが率いた連合国軍が、そして他方にはドイツ率いる同盟国軍がありました。

　多くのアメリカ人はフランスとイギリスに同情しながらも、大西洋を隔てて戦闘のない平和な国で生活していることをありがたく思っていました。彼らは、中立を保ち、参戦しないというアメリカ政府の決断を支持していました。しかし、一連の出来事がアメリカ人の怒りを買い、参戦に向かわせたのです。

Vocabulary

☐ be separated from 　～から隔たる 　　☐ neutral 　中立の
☐ enter 　入る

Sinking of the *Lusitania*

One of those was the sinking of the British passenger ship *Lusitania*, which was traveling from New York City to Britain in 1914. It was attacked with torpedoes by a German U-boat, a submarine, and over one thousand civilian men, women, and children were killed. Over one hundred of those were Americans.

In early 1917, the German government announced it would instruct U-boat captains to sink any ship sailing toward England from the United States and other countries. Germany also sent a telegram to the Mexican government, offering a secret deal. If Mexico would join the German and the other Central Powers, Germany would help Mexico regain territories in the United States that Mexico had lost in the Mexican-American War.

End of World War I

In April 1917, President Woodrow Wilson asked Congress to declare war on Germany. Congress voted to agree with Wilson, and America began training soldiers to fight against Germany. After a long, deadly conflict, Germany was defeated and the Allies won. The shooting stopped in November 1918.

Let's try it!

Q79 Who was President during World War I?

→ Answer p.155

ルシタニア号の沈没

　その 1 つの出来事が、1914 年にニューヨークからイギリスに向かって航行していたイギリスの客船、ルシタニア号の沈没でした。ドイツの潜水艦、U ボートの魚雷により攻撃され、1,000 人以上の一般の男性、女性、そして子どもが亡くなりました。その犠牲者のうち、100 人以上がアメリカ人でした。

　1917 年初頭、ドイツ政府はアメリカやその他の国からイギリスに向かうすべての船を撃沈するよう、U ボートの艦長たちに指示することを発表しました。また、ドイツはメキシコ政府に密約を持ち掛ける電報を打ちました。メキシコがドイツをはじめ同盟国側に加われば、ドイツはメキシコに、アメリカ・メキシコ戦争（米墨戦争）でメキシコが失った領土の奪還に力を貸すと申し入れたのです。

第一次世界大戦終結

　1917 年 4 月、ウッドロー・ウィルソン大統領がドイツとの戦争を宣言するよう議会に求めました。議会はウィルソンに同意し、アメリカはドイツとの戦いに向けて兵士の訓練を始めました。長く命がけの戦いの末、ドイツが敗北し、連合国軍が勝利しました。1918 年の 11 月に戦火は止みました。

Vocabulary

- ☐ passenger　乗客、船客
- ☐ U-boat　（世界大戦での）潜水艦
- ☐ telegram　電報
- ☐ deadly　致命的な、死をもたらす
- ☐ torpedo　魚雷
- ☐ civilian　一般人の、一般市民の
- ☐ declare　宣言する
- ☐ shooting　狙撃、殺し合うこと

26 The Great Depression

In the 1920s, the American economy boomed. Many Americans had conveniences and a comfortable lifestyle with electric lights, new home appliances, and gasoline-powered automobiles. Businessman Henry Ford began to manufacture a car called the Model T which was well built and cheap enough for the average person to buy. Life seemed easy.

But American industry grew too rapidly and there were more products than people could afford to buy. In addition, people got into the habit of spending more money than they had. They began to borrow money to pay for what they bought. As a result, people went into debt. When they had well-paying jobs, they could easily pay off their debts and still enjoy what they bought. But when companies began to fire workers, it created a spiral. People had debts, but no paying jobs to enable them to pay off the debts. Americans stopped buying new things, factories shut down, workers lost their jobs, and suddenly millions of Americans were struggling to survive.

When the stock market crashed in 1929, America entered the Great Depression, the longest economic recession in modern history. From the Great Crash of 1929 through the 1930s, the economic situation grew worse and worse, and many Americans gave up hope of a brighter future.

大恐慌

　1920 年代、アメリカ経済は好景気に沸いていました。多くのアメリカ人は電灯や新しい家電製品のある家に住み、ガソリンで動く自動車を使って、快適な暮らしを手に入れました。実業家のヘンリー・フォードが T 型と呼ばれる自動車を製造し始めました。これは頑丈な造りで、一般の人でも買うことができました。暮らしは楽になったように思えました。

　しかし、アメリカの産業はあまりにも急速に成長しすぎて、人々が購入できるよりも多くの製品が製造されていました。さらに、人々は自分達が実際に持っている以上のお金を使う習慣を身に付けてしまいました。人々はものを購入したものの、支払いのためお金を借りるようになったのです。その結果、人々は負債を抱えることになりました。稼ぎの良い仕事があったときは、簡単に借金を返済でき、購入したものを楽しむことができましたが、企業が従業員を解雇し始めると、悪循環（負のスパイラル）に陥っていきました。人々は負債を抱えましたが、返済するためにお金を稼ぎたくても仕事はありませんでした。アメリカの人々は新しいものを買わなくなり、工場は閉鎖し、労働者は仕事を失い、突然何百万人ものアメリカ人が生活に苦労するようになったのです。

　1929 年に株式市場が大暴落すると、アメリカは大恐慌に突入し、近代史上最も長い経済不況となりました。「1929 年の大暴落」から 1930 年代を通して景気はどんどん悪化し、多くのアメリカ人はより明るい未来への希望を捨てました。

Vocabulary

- □ boom　景気づく
- □ afford　（ものを買う）余裕を持つ
- □ spiral　（物価、資金などの）悪循環によるラセン状進行過程
- □ conveniences　便利なもの
- □ debt　借金
- □ recession　不景気、不況

133

27 The New Deal

When Franklin Delano Roosevelt (FDR) became president in 1933, his "New Deal" policies helped to lift the United States out of the Great Depression. The government created jobs for young men to work on projects to improve national parks and stop soil erosion in the nation's forests and farmlands. The government also built new roads, bridges, power plants, schools, hospitals, and airports. It also created Social Security, a program that supported people if they lost their jobs or if they were unable to work due to age or illness.

Let's try it!

Q80 Who was President during the Great Depression and World War II?

→ Answer p.155

ニューディール

　1933 年にフランクリン・デラノ・ルーズベルト（FDR）が大統領に就任すると、彼の「ニューディール」政策のおかげでアメリカは大恐慌から抜け出しました。政府は国立公園を整備したり、国の森林や農地の土壌侵食を食い止めるプロジェクトに従事する若者の雇用を作り出しました。また、政府は新しい道路、橋、発電所、学校、病院、そして空港を建設しました。さらに社会保障制度という、労働者が職を失ったり、年齢や病気によって働けなくなった際に保障を受けられるプログラムも作りました。

Vocabulary

- [ ] lift　引き上げる、抜け出す
- [ ] power plant　発電所、発電設備
- [ ] due to　～による
- [ ] erosion　浸食（作用）
- [ ] Social Security　（米）社会保障

28 World War II (1939-1945)

While America was gradually recovering, however, Germany was once again moving to conquer the world. Germany allied itself with Italy and Japan to form the Axis Powers. In the United States, the majority of people sympathized with Britain's lonely fight against  Germany. But few Americans were eager to go to war again. President Roosevelt, however, convinced Congress to build up its defenses and also become "the arsenal of democracy" making ships, planes, and tanks to help Britain.

America entered the war following the Japanese attack on Pearl Harbor on December 7, 1941. (America had not prepared to actually fight until then, so the December 7 attack on Pearl Harbor was the trigger for going to war.) The day after the attack, President Roosevelt asked Congress to declare war on Japan.

第二次世界大戦

　アメリカは徐々に回復に向かっていましたが、その間、ドイツは再び世界を征服するために動き出していました。ドイツはイタリアと日本と枢軸国として同盟を組みました。アメリカでは、大多数の人がイギリスのドイツに対する孤独な戦いに同情的でした。ただ、再び戦争に行きたがる人はほとんどいませんでした。しかし、ルーズベルト大統領はアメリカは国防を強化し、船舶、飛行機、戦車を製造してイギリスを援助する「民主主義の武器庫」になるよう議会を説得しました。

　アメリカが実際に戦争に加わったのは、日本が1941年12月7日（日本時間では12月8日）に真珠湾を攻撃したときでした（それまでアメリカはまだ戦う準備が整っておらず、実際に戦争に踏み切ったのは12月7日の真珠湾攻撃がきっかけでした）。攻撃の翌日、ルーズベルト大統領は議会に、日本への宣戦布告を要請しました。

Several days later, Japan's allies, Germany and Italy, declared war on the United States. America was once again involved in a world war, this time it was called World War II. America supported the Allied Powers whose members were England, France, and Russia against the Axis Powers.

America and the other Allied Powers were victors at the end of World War II. By the end of the war, Roosevelt died and Harry Truman became president. Among the important military figures that emerged from the war was the American General Dwight Eisenhower, who led the Allied forces on D-Day, June 6, 1944. Eisenhower later became President of the United States.

☼ *Let's try it!*

Q81 Who did the United States fight in World War II?

Q82 Before he was President, (Dwight) Eisenhower was a general. What war was he in?

→ Answer p.155

　数日後、日本の同盟国であるドイツとイタリアがアメリカに宣戦布告しました。アメリカは再び世界戦争に巻き込まれることになったのです。この戦争は第二次世界大戦と呼ばれました。アメリカは、イギリス、フランス、ソ連の連合国軍を支持し、枢軸国との戦いに加わりました。

　第二次世界大戦の終結で勝利したのはアメリカを含む連合国軍でした。戦争の終わるころにはルーズベルトは亡くなり、ハリー・トルーマンが大統領に就任しました。この戦争から生まれた重要な軍事的人物のなかには、1944年のDデイ（6月6日）に連合国軍の指揮をとっていたアメリカの将軍、ドワイト・アイゼンハワーがいました。アイゼンハワーは後にアメリカの大統領となりました。

Vocabulary ....

☐ sympathize with　〜に同情する　　　☐ be eager to　〜したがる、〜に前むきである

☐ arsenal　兵器工場、倉庫　　　　　　　☐ declare war (on)　（〜に）宣戦布告する

☐ axis　軸、（第二次世界大戦の）日独伊枢軸国

29 The Cold War

When World War II came to an end, the United States and the Soviet Union were the most powerful countries in the world. They were called "superpowers." They had overlooked their political and economic system differences and fought together as allies, but once the war ended, they quickly became enemies.

They engaged in a long period of tense hostility called "the Cold War" from 1946 to 1991. Several times they came dangerously close to a "hot" war, that would have involved bombing and bullets.

One of those times was when American troops fought against Communist forces in Korea. After World War II, the southern part of Korea was occupied by the United States, and the northern part was occupied by the Soviet Union.

Let's try it!

> **Q83** During the Cold War, what was one main concern of the United States?

→ Answer p.155

冷戦

　第二次世界大戦が終結したころ、アメリカとソ連は「超大国」と呼ばれ、世界で最も強力な国家でした。政治体制、経済体制の違いには目を瞑り、連合国として共に戦いましたが、戦争が終わるとすぐに敵対しました。

　両国は、1946年から1991年にわたり、「冷戦」と呼ばれる長く張りつめた敵対関係が続きました。何度か爆撃や銃弾を伴う「熱い」戦争に危険なほど近づいたこともありました。

　そのうちの1つが、アメリカ軍が朝鮮で共産主義勢力と戦ったときです。第二次世界大戦後、朝鮮半島の南部はアメリカが占領し、北部はソ連が占領していました。

Vocabulary

□ engage in 　〜に参加する　　　　□ be occupied by 　〜によって占領される

30 The Korean War

In June 1950, the North Korean (the Democratic People's Republic of Korea) army invaded South Korea (the Republic of Korea). To prevent the spread of communism, American troops landed in South Korea and began pushing North Korean troops back into North Korea. This was the beginning of the Korean War. The American troops pushed the North Korean troops all the way to the Chinese border. Then Communist China joined the war. The possibility of an attack on China leading to war with the Soviet Union, which might involve nuclear weapons, was real.

In the end, Chinese troops drove the American troops back to the border between North and South Korea, and in 1953 a truce was signed. There was no clear-cut victory. But there had been no nuclear war either.

1950年6月、北朝鮮（朝鮮民主主義人民共和国）の軍隊は韓国（大韓民国）に侵攻しました。共産主義が広まるのを防ぐため、アメリカ軍は韓国に上陸し、北朝鮮軍を北朝鮮国内に追撃しました。これが朝鮮戦争の始まりでした。アメリカ軍は北朝鮮軍を中国との国境にまで追撃し、ここで共産主義国家の中国が参戦したのです。中国への攻撃がソ連との戦争を誘発し、核兵器の使用が現実味を帯びました。

最終的に、中国軍はアメリカ軍を南北朝鮮の国境まで押し戻し、1953年には停戦協定が結ばれました。明確な勝利はなかったものの、核戦争は回避できたのです。

TO HONOR ALL
WHO SERVED
KOREAN WAR
1950 — 1953

Vocabulary

- [ ] invade　侵攻する
- [ ] truce　休戦、戦闘停止
- [ ] clear-cut　明確な
- [ ] nuclear weapon　核兵器
- [ ] sign　承認する、署名する

31 The Civil Rights Movement

During the 1950s and 1960s, the Civil Rights Movement worked to end discrimination against Black people in the United States. Blacks were not treated equally in the workplace, in schools, on public transportation, and in federal and state elections.

The most famous leader in the movement was the African American minister Dr. Martin Luther King, Jr. (King received a Ph.D. from Boston University and is therefore called Dr. King.) He and other leaders led peaceful protests and demonstrations to support new Civil Rights laws. In 1963 they led the March on Washington. During that demonstration in Washington, D.C., Dr. King delivered his powerful "I Have a Dream" speech.

Their activities led to new Civil Rights Acts (guaranteeing equality in choosing a place to live, voting in elections, and receiving education), aimed at improving the treatment of people of color. In other words, he worked for equality for all Americans.

Dr. King was assassinated in 1968 and the United States commemorates his birthday as a national holiday on the third Monday in January in honor of his lifetime contributions.

Let's try it!

Q84 What movement tried to end racial discrimination?

Q85 What did Martin Luther King, Jr., do?

→ Answer p.155

公民権運動

1950年代から1960年代にかけて、アメリカでの黒人差別を終わらせるための公民権運動が起きました。黒人は職場、学校、公共交通機関、連邦および州の選挙において平等に扱われていませんでした。

この運動で最も有名な指導者が、アフリカ系アメリカ人牧師であるマーティン・ルーサー・キング博士でした（キングはボストン大学で修士号（Ph.D.）を取得したため、「ドクター」キングと呼ばれます）。キングをはじめとした指導者たちは、新しい公民権法を支持するため、平和的な抗議運動やデモ行進を導きました。1963年、ワシントンで行われた行進で、キング牧師は有名な「私には夢がある」の力強い演説を行ったのです。

彼らの活動は、有色人種の待遇改善（平等な居住権、選挙権、教育を受ける権利を保障する）を目的とした公民権法という新しい法律の制定につながりました。つまり、彼はすべてのアメリカ人の平等のために尽力したのです。

キング牧師は1968年に暗殺されましたが、アメリカでは彼の生涯の功績を称え、1月の第3月曜日に彼の誕生日を祝日としています。

Vocabulary

- ☐ demonstration　デモ
- ☐ people of color　有色人種
- ☐ contribution　貢献
- ☐ march　デモ行進
- ☐ assassinate　暗殺する

32 Native American Movement

The Civil Rights Movement had an impact on minorities including the Native Americans. Stimulated by the African American movement for respect and equal rights, Native Americans became more vocal in demanding redress for the injustices they had suffered for centuries.

The most significant event in the Native Americans' movement occurred along Wounded Knee Creek, in South Dakota. It was the site of an earlier tragedy, in 1890, in which a band of 250 Lakota Sioux were killed by federal troops. Wounded Knee became a focal point of the Native American protesters in 1973, where they called for the right to manage their own reservation affairs, to protect their natural resources from non-Indian exploitation, to protect treaty rights and to end poverty.

The one positive result of the demonstrations at Wounded Knee was an improved recognition of treaty rights and a recognition of the rights of Native Americans to determine how they chose to live and how they were to govern their communities. A new law in 1975 allowed tribes to contract with the government to develop their own human resources—health, education, social service—and law enforcement programs. Other rights were put into federal law.

アメリカ先住民の運動

　公民権運動は先住民など、その他のマイノリティにも影響を与えました。アフリカ系アメリカ人による敬意と平等な権利のための活動に刺激を受け、アメリカ先住民は何世紀にもわたって受けてきた不当な扱いに対して救済を求める声を強めました。

　この運動で最も重要な出来事は、サウスダコタ州のウンデッド・ニー・クリーク（小川）で起きました。そこは 1890 年に 250 人ものラコタ・スー族の一団が連邦軍によって殺された悲劇の場所でした。1973 年、ウンデッド・ニーはアメリカ先住民の抗議活動の中心地となりました。そこで彼らは、居留地を自ら管理する権利、天然資源を外部の搾取から守ること、条約上の権利を守ること、そして貧困を終わらせることについて訴えました。

　ウンデッド・ニーでの抗議運動で生まれた成果の 1 つは、条約上の権利と、アメリカ先住民がどのように生活し、コミュニティを統治するかを自ら決める権利に対する認識が改善したことです。1975 年には新しい法律が制定され、先住民の部族は自らの健康、教育、社会事業に関する人的資源および法の執行プログラムの開発に対し、政府と契約できるようになりました。他の権利については連邦法で規定されました。

Vocabulary

- □ vocal　言葉に表す
- □ injustice　不公平な行為
- □ recognition　公認
- □ redress　救済、改善
- □ exploitation　不当な扱い、搾取
- □ law enforcement　法執行（機関）

33 Women's Liberation Movement

Beginning in the nineteenth century, American women struggled to win basic rights like the right to vote, equal education, and equal pay for equal jobs in the workplace. During World War II, many American women took jobs in offices and factories that made use of their skills. They were eager to actively participate in society and use their talents and interests.

When World War II ended and men came home from the military, women lost their places in society.

In the 1960s and 1970s the feminist movement was reborn in America. It promoted the idea that women should have the same rights and opportunities as men in all fields and have equal legal standing in the law and the workplace.

女性解放運動

　19世紀から、アメリカの女性たちは選挙権、平等な教育、職場での平等な賃金や雇用の均等などの基本的権利を勝ち取るために奮闘してきました。第二次世界大戦中、多くのアメリカ人女性たちは職場や工場でスキルを生かした仕事に就いていました。より積極的に社会に参加し、才能や興味を活かしたかったのです。

　ところが第二次世界大戦が終わり、男性が軍隊から帰還すると、女性は社会での居場所を失いました。

　1960年代から1970年代にかけて、フェミニズム運動がアメリカで再燃しました。女性が男性とすべての分野において同じ権利や機会を有し、法律や職場でも同等の法的地位を持つべきだと主張しました。

Vocabulary

□ workplace　職場
□ reborn　よみがえる、生まれかわる
□ talent　才能
□ legal standing　法的立場

34 Vietnam War / Persian Gulf War

Vietnam War

Vietnam was once a colony of France, but when the French withdrew, the country divided into two countries, the communist north and the non-communist south. The north began training fighters to overthrow the south. Beginning in 1964 the United States sent "advisers" to train and advise southern Vietnamese troops. Eventually America became more involved in actually fighting against the northern army. American troops withdrew in 1973 and the northern Vietnamese army took control of the whole country.

Persian Gulf War

The Persian Gulf War began when Iraq invaded Kuwait in 1990. The United States entered the war in 1991 in order to force the Iraqi military from Kuwait. A coalition of armed forces from 34 nations pushed the Iraq forces out of Kuwait in 1991. America also referred to the Persian Gulf War as Operation Desert Storm.

Let's try it!

Q78 **Name one war fought by the United States in the 1900s.**

→ Answer p.155

ベトナム戦争 / ペルシャ湾戦争

ベトナム戦争

　ベトナムはかつてフランスの植民地でした。しかしフランスが撤退した後、共産主義の北部と非共産主義の南部の2つの国に分かれ、北は南を打倒するために戦闘員の訓練を開始しました。1964年からアメリカは「アドバイザー」を派遣して南ベトナム軍の訓練と助言を行い、やがて北軍との実際の戦闘に関与を深めるようになりました。そして1973年、アメリカ軍は撤退し、ベトナム北部軍が全土を支配するようになりました。

ペルシャ湾戦争（湾岸戦争）

　ペルシャ湾戦争は、1990年にイラクがクウェートを侵攻したのをきっかけに始まりました。アメリカ合衆国は、1991年にクウェートからイラク軍を撤退させようとして参戦しました。1991年に、34カ国の諸国連合から結成された多国籍軍がイラク軍をクウェートから追い出しました。アメリカはこの戦争を"Operation Desert Storm（砂漠の嵐作戦）"とも呼びました。

Vocabulary

- □ invade　侵攻する
- □ coalition　連合
- □ military　軍
- □ armed forces　軍隊

35 September 11, 2001

On the morning of September 11, 2001, terrorists attacked the United States in several places. The terrorists hijacked four airplanes and used them to destroy important locations in America.

One plane failed to reach its target in Washington, D.C., and crashed in a field in Pennsylvania.

A second plane crashed into the Pentagon, the headquarters of the United States armed forces in Arlington, Virginia.

Two other planes crashed into the twin towers of the World Trade Center in Manhattan in New York City.

At almost the same time, thousands of people died in the buildings and on the airplanes. They included people from over eighty countries, and most of the victims were American.

The United States government called on other nations to join in a global "War on Terror." President George W. Bush then sent American troops to Afghanistan to fight against the terrorist organization responsible for the attacks.

The U.S. military continued conflicts in what became known as the War in Afghanistan and the War in Iraq.

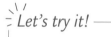

Let's try it!

Q86 **What major event happened on September 11, 2001, in the United States?**

→ Answer p.155

9.11 米国同時多発テロ

2001年9月11日の朝、テロリストがアメリカ各地を攻撃しました。テロリストは4機の旅客機をハイジャックし、アメリカ各地の重要拠点を破壊したのです。

そのうちの1機はワシントンD.C.に向かっていましたが、標的に到達せず、ペンシルベニア州の草原に墜落。

2機目はバージニア州アーリントンにあるアメリカ国防総省の本庁舎ペンタゴンに墜落。

他の2機はニューヨークのマンハッタンにあるワールド・トレード・センターのツインタワーに激突。

これらはほぼ同時に起き、飛行機と建物の中で何千人もの人が犠牲となりました。犠牲者の国籍は約80カ国におよびますが、犠牲者の多くはアメリカ人でした。

アメリカ政府は他の国々に、対テロ戦争（テロとのグローバル戦争）に加わるよう呼びかけ、ジョージ・W・ブッシュ大統領はこの攻撃を起こしたテロ組織と戦うためアメリカ軍をアフガニスタンに派兵しました。

アメリカ軍はアフガン戦争とイラク戦争として知られるようになった紛争を続けました。

Vocabulary

☐ terrorist　テロリスト
☐ headquarter(s)　本部
☐ location　場所
☐ victim　犠牲者

Let's Try Test Questions

Page 130 **Q 79** Who was President during World War I?

Page 134 **Q 80** Who was President during the Great Depression and World War II?

Page 138 **Q 81** Who did the United States fight in World War II?

Q 82 Before he was President, (Dwight) Eisenhower was a general. What war was he in?

Page 140 **Q 83** During the Cold War, what was one main concern of the United States?

Page 144 **Q 84** What movement tried to end racial discrimination?

Q 85 What did Martin Luther King, Jr., do?

Page 150 **Q 78** Name one war fought by the United States in the 1900s.

Page 152 **Q 86** What major event happened on September 11, 2001, in the United States?

Answers

A79 第一次世界大戦中の大統領は誰でしたか？
(Woodrow) Wilson （ウッドロー）ウィルソン

A80 大恐慌と第二次世界大戦の時の大統領は誰でしたか？
(Franklin) Roosevelt （フランクリン）ルーズベルト

A81 アメリカは第二次世界大戦で誰と戦いましたか？
Japan, Germany, and Italy 日本、ドイツ、およびイタリア

A82 （ドワイト）アイゼンハワーは大統領就任前は司令官でした。どの戦争の司令官でしたか？
World War II 第二次世界大戦

A83 冷戦中にアメリカが主に懸念していたことの1つは何でしたか？
Communism 共産主義

A84 人種差別を終わらせようとした運動は何ですか？
Civil rights (movement) 　公民権（運動）

A85 マーティン・ルーサー・キング・ジュニアは何をした人物ですか？
Fought for civil rights 公民権のために闘った , **Worked for equality for all Americans** すべてのアメリカ市民の平等のために活動した

A78 アメリカ合衆国が1900年代に戦った戦争を1つ挙げてください。
World War I 第一次世界大戦 , **World War II** 第二次世界大戦 , **Korean War** 朝鮮戦争 , **Vietnam War** ベトナム戦争 , **Persian Gulf War** ペルシャ湾戦争（湾岸戦争）

A86 2001年9月11日にアメリカで起きた大きな出来事は何ですか？
Terrorists attacked the United States. テロリストがアメリカを攻撃した

Lincoln's second inaugural, 1865

Part 3

U.S. Government and Civics

アメリカ政府と公民

1 Laws

The United States is a republic. It has a democratic form of government, which is a representative form of government. The American people vote for public officials who serve the American people.

The fundamental principle of American democracy is called the "rule of law." This means that the people, the leaders, and the government must obey the law. In other words, no one is above the law.

☀ *Let's try it!* ─────────────────────────────

Q12 **What is the "rule of law"?**

→ Answer p.201

法

アメリカは「共和国」です。つまり、選出された代表者がその権力を行使する民主政体（民主主義政府）です。アメリカの国民は、アメリカ国民に奉仕する公務員に投票します。

民主主義の基本原理は「法の支配」です。一般の市民（国民）であれ、指導者であれ、政府であれ、法を守らなければいけません。つまり、どのような個人でも法を超越することはないのです。

Vocabulary

☐ republic　共和国
☐ fundamental　基本的な

☐ serve　〜のために働く

2 The U.S. Constitution

When the American colonies declared their independence from Britain, the Constitution of the United States was the result of long discussions between representatives of the various colonies who met in Philadelphia.

The Constitution is the fundamental law of the United States. It establishes the organization of the government, defines the power of each part of the government, and establishes the rights of American citizens. It is not based on religion or traditional monarchy. It begins with a statement of self-government: "We the People."

Today Americans have varying interpretations of the rights and obligations of the Constitution but it remains the most important document in American society.

⟅Let's try it!

Q 2 What does the Constitution do?

Q 3 The idea of self-government is in the first three words of the Constitution. What are these words?

→ Answer p.201

アメリカの植民地がイギリスからの独立を宣言したとき、フィラデルフィア
に集まった各植民地の代表者が長い間協議した末に生まれたのが合衆国憲法
です。

憲法はアメリカの基本法です。政府の組織を定め、政府の各部の権限を定義
し、アメリカ市民の権利を確立しますが、それは宗教や伝統的な王制に基づく
ものではありません。憲法は「われら国民は」という自治の表明で始まります。

今日、アメリカ人は憲法の権利と義務について様々な解釈をしていますが、
憲法がアメリカ社会において最も重要な文書であることに変わりはありませ
ん。

3 The Bill of Rights

The supreme law of the country is the U.S. Constitution. This includes the Bill of Rights, which are the first ten amendments to the Constitution. They were added to the Constitution in 1791 and they protect the basic rights of American citizens and non-citizens.

The First Amendment protects freedom of religion, speech, press, assembly, and petition. It guarantees the separation of church (religion) and state (government). It protects the right to petition the government.

- Freedom of speech (freedom of thought and opinion) means that Americans can say what they want to.
- Freedom of the press (freedom of thought and expression) means that Americans can write what they want to.
- Freedom of religion means that Americans can practice any religion, or not practice a religion. It is up to each individual to choose.

The Second Amendment protects the right to bear arms.

The Third Amendment protects against the forced quartering of troops in one's home.

The Fourth Amendment protects against unreasonable search and seizures of property.

The Fifth Amendment protects the legal rights of citizens. No one can be deprived of life, liberty, or property without due process of law.

権利章典

　アメリカ合衆国の最高法規は憲法です。その修正条項の最初の 10 条は権利章典と呼ばれており、アメリカ市民および非市民の基本的権利を守るために 1971 年に憲法に追加されました。

　憲法修正第 1 条は宗教、言論、出版、集会の自由、そして請願権を守ります。政教分離原則（宗教と政治機関・国・国家を切り離すこと）が保障され、政府に請願する権利を守ります。

- 言論の自由は、アメリカ人が自由に（意見や思想を）発言できることを意味します。
- 出版の自由は、アメリカ人が（意見や思想を）自由に書けることを意味します。
- 宗教の自由とは、アメリカ人が宗教を信仰する（そしてその信仰の活動や行為を行う）、または信仰しない自由のことです。個人それぞれの選択です。

　憲法修正第 2 条は、武器を保有し携行する権利を保障します。

　憲法修正第 3 条は、個人の家に承諾なく強制的に軍隊を宿営させることを禁止します。

　憲法修正第 4 条は、不当な財産の捜索や押収から保護します。

　憲法修正第 5 条は、国民の法的権利を守ります。法の適切な手続きを取らずに生命、自由または財産を奪われることはありません。

The Sixth Amendment guarantees a fair and trial by an impartial jury. It guarantees representation by a lawyer.

The Seventh Amendment protects the right to a trial by a jury in civil cases involving common law.

The Eighth Amendment protects against excessive bail, excessive fines, and cruel and unusual punishment.

The Ninth Amendment guarantees certain rights, including the right to privacy in American homes. Police need a special document from a court before they can go into a person's home.

The Tenth Amendment says that powers not delegated by the Constitution to the national government, nor prohibited by it to the states, are reserved to the states or to the people.

Let's try it! —————————————————————

Ⓠ① What is the supreme law of the land?

Ⓠ④ What is an amendment?

Ⓠ⑤ What do we call the first ten amendments to the Constitution?

Ⓠ⑥ What is one right or freedom from the First Amendment?

→ Answer p.201

憲法修正第 **6** 条は、公平な陪審による裁判を保障します。弁護人による代理を保障します。

憲法修正第 **7** 条は、コモン・ロー（普通法）上の民事訴訟において、陪審による裁判を受ける権利を守ります。

憲法修正第 **8** 条は、過大な額の保釈金、過大な刑罰、そして残酷で異常な刑罰から守ります。

憲法修正第 **9** 条は、国民の保有する土地におけるプライバシーの権利を含む、一定の権利を保障します。警察が国民の住まいに入るには裁判所からの特別な許可書が必要です。

憲法修正第 **10** 条は、憲法が連邦政府に委任していない、または州に対して禁止していない権限は、州または国民に留保されるとしています。

Vocabulary

☐ assembly　集会
☐ bear arms　武器を持つ
☐ seizure　差し押さえ
☐ punishment　罰、刑

☐ petition　請願（する）
☐ practice religion　宗教の教えを信じる
☐ impartial　公平な

---

4 Balance of Powers

The founders of the country, who did not want to see power gathered in one place—as it tended to be in Britain—devised what is called the "balance of powers." This system divided the government into three elements, which are called the executive branch, the legislative branch, and the judicial branch, therefore dividing power and authority. This is a system of checks and balances. It stops one branch of government from becoming too powerful.

The executive branch is composed of the Presidency. This means the U.S. President, the Vice President, and the Cabinet officers.

The legislative branch is composed of a two-part Congress. This means the U.S. Senate and the U.S. House of Representatives.

The judicial branch is composed of the federal courts and the U.S. Supreme Court at the top.

The three branches of the government are located in Washington, D.C.

Let's try it!

Q13　Name one branch or part of the government.

Q14　What stops one branch of government from becoming too powerful?

→ Answer p.201

権力の分立（三権分立）

　アメリカ建国の父たちは、イギリスのように権力が1カ所に集中するのを避けるため、権力の分立（三権分立）の制度を考案しました。このシステムでは政府を行政府、立法府、そして司法府の3つの部門に分け、権力を分散させました。これはチェックアンドバランス（権力の抑制と均衡）という制度で、いずれかの部門が強力になりすぎることを防ぎます。

　行政府は大統領職から成り立ちます。つまり、大統領、副大統領、そして（各省庁の）官僚を指します。

　立法府は2つの議会から成り立ちます。上院と下院の二院制議会です。

　司法府は最高裁判所を頂点とする複数の連邦裁判所から成り立ちます。

　この3つの部門はワシントン D.C. にあります。

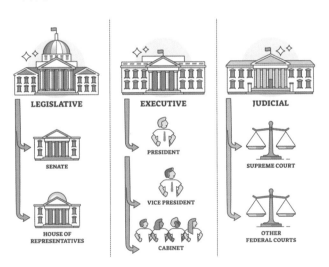

Vocabulary

- [ ] executive　行政府、行政機関
- [ ] judicial　司法府、司法機関
- [ ] be composed of　〜によって形成されている
- [ ] legislative　立法府、立法機関
- [ ] branches (of government)　（政府の）部門

5 The Presidency (The White House)

The President, Vice President, and the Cabinet are often referred to as "the White House" in news media.

What does the President do? The President enforces the laws of the United States. He or she is called the chief executive and is also the Commander-in-Chief of the military.

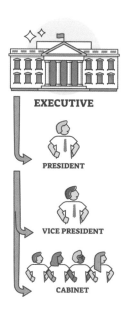

The President is elected for a term of four years. The President can serve two terms.

To become President, a person must be a natural-born citizen of the United States. That means he or she must be born in the United States. The person must also be at least 35 years old. The person must live in the United States for at least 14 years before serving as President.

What does the Vice President do? The Vice President works with the President, and if the President can no longer serve, the Vice President automatically becomes the President. If neither the President nor Vice President is able to fulfill the duties of the Presidency, the Speaker of the House of Representatives automatically assumes that position.

The American people elect the President and the Vice President at the same time, in November of the election year. Both of the elected take office in January of the following year.

大統領府（ホワイトハウス）

ニュースメディアでは大統領、副大統領、および内閣（大統領顧問団）のことを"the White House（ホワイトハウス）"と呼びます。

大統領の役割は何でしょうか？ 大統領は法案に署名して法律を施行します。行政部の最高責任者とも呼ばれ、軍の最高司令官でもあります。

大統領の任期は4年で、2期（8年）まで務められます。

大統領になるには、生まれながらのアメリカ国民であることが必要です。つまり、アメリカで生まれていなければなりません。また、35歳以上でなければなりません。さらに、大統領就任前に14年以上アメリカに住んでいなければなりません。

副大統領の役割は何でしょうか？ 副大統領は大統領と共に職務にあたります。大統領が（死亡、辞任などによって）任務を果たせなくなったとき、副大統領が自動的に大統領になります。大統領も副大統領もその職務につけなくなったときは、下院議長が自動的にその職につきます。

大統領と副大統領は、選挙の年の11月に国民によって同時に選出され、翌年の1月に就任します。

What does the Cabinet do? The President's Cabinet advises the President. Each member represents a department of the federal bureaucracy and raises issues from each department to the Cabinet.

Cabinet-level positions include the following:

The Secretary of **Agriculture**	The Secretary of **Commerce**	The Secretary of **Defense**
The Secretary of **Education**	The Secretary of **Energy**	The Secretary of **Health and Human Services**
The Secretary of **Homeland Security**	The Secretary of **Housing and Urban Development**	The Secretary of **the Interior**
The Secretary of **Labor**	The Secretary of **State**	The Secretary of **Transportation**
The Secretary of **the Treasury**	The Secretary of **Veterans Affairs**	**The Attorney General**
The Vice President		

☀ Let's try it!

Q15 Who is in charge of the executive branch?

Q26 We elect a President for how many years?

Q27 In what month do we vote for President?

Q28 What is the name of the President of the United States now?

Q29 What is the name of the Vice President of the United States now?

Q30 If the President can no longer serve, who becomes President?

Q31 If both the President and the Vice President can no longer serve, who becomes President?

Q32 Who is the Commander-in-Chief of the military?

Q33 Who signs bills to become laws?

Q35 What does the President's Cabinet do?

Q36 What are two Cabinet-level positions?

→ Answer p.201、203

内閣（大統領顧問団）の役割は何でしょうか？ 大統領の諮問機関である内閣は大統領に助言します。各省の長官から成るメンバーたちはそれぞれの省を代表し、各部門に関連する問題について内閣に提起します。

内閣の役職には以下のものがあります：

農務長官	商務長官	国防長官
教育長官	エネルギー長官	保健福祉長官
国土安全保障長官	住宅都市開発長官	内務長官
労働長官	国務長官	運輸長官
財務長官	退役軍人長官	司法長官
副大統領		

6 The Electoral College

The presidential electors are a group who meet after the citizens vote for the president and vice president in the national election. Each state is given the same number of electors as it has Senators and Representatives combined. In other words, it is these electors—rather than the public—that actually elect the president and vice president.

The Founding Fathers believed that the electors would exercise discretion, and would not necessarily be bound by the popular vote. But the rise of political parties changed that belief. Electors are now pledged in advance to vote for the candidate of their party. They almost always do that. The vote of the Electoral College is, therefore, largely a formality.

There have been several attempts to abolish the Electoral College system.

選挙人団

選挙人団は、国民が国政選挙で大統領と副大統領に投票した後に集まります。各州には、その州選出の下院議員と上院議員の数の合計と同じ数の選挙人がいます。つまり、実際に大統領と副大統領を選んでいるのは有権者ではなく、選挙人なのです。

建国の父たちは、選挙人たちが一般投票に縛られず、裁量権を行使すると信じていました。しかし、政党が台頭するにつれ、その考え方は変わりました。現在、選挙人はあらかじめそれぞれの所属する政党に投票するよう誓約しなければなりません。そして実際のところ、ほとんどの場合はそうします。よって、選挙人団の投票はほぼ形式的なものとなっているのです。

過去には、このような選挙人団のシステムを廃止しようとする動きが何度かありました。

Vocabulary

- ☐ elector　選挙人
- ☐ discretion　裁量、慎重な行動
- ☐ abolish　廃止する
- ☐ the public　国民、大衆
- ☐ formality　形式的であること

7 America's Political Parties

The two main political parties are the Democratic Party, symbolized by the donkey, and the Republican Party, symbolized by the elephant. It has recently become common to use the color "red" for the Republicans and "blue" for the Democrats, especially in reference to "red states" and "blue states" where one party is dominant. States that are not clearly one or the other are often colored purple on maps.

Presidents like Clinton, Obama, and Biden were Democrats. Presidents like Bush and Trump were Republican.

States on the northeast Atlantic Coast including New York and New England and on the Pacific Coast including California have tended to be run by Democratic Congress members, governors, and mayors. Their policies tend toward raising taxes to pay for welfare and to help minorities and relieve poverty. States from Florida to Texas and into the middle of America have tended to elect Republican candidates. Their policies tend toward lowering taxes, giving benefits to businesses, and opposing migrants.

Let's try it!

Q45 What are the two major political parties in the United States?

Q46 What is the political party of the President now?

→ Answer p.203

アメリカの政党

　アメリカにおける2大政党は、ロバに象徴される民主党と、象に象徴される共和党です。最近では、共和党に「赤」、民主党に「青」を使用することが一般的で、特にそれぞれの政党が優勢な州を表現するとき、「赤い州」「青い州」と呼びます。そしてどちらが優勢かはっきりしない州は地図で紫色に表示されます。

　クリントン、オバマ、バイデン大統領は民主党、ブッシュ、トランプ大統領は共和党でした。

　ニューヨーク州やニューイングランド州など大西洋岸北東部、およびカリフォルニア州など太平洋岸にある州は民主党の議員や知事、市長が運営する傾向にあり、その政策は福祉や少数民族の救済、貧困の解消のために増税する傾向にあります。一方、フロリダからテキサス、そしてアメリカ中部の州では、共和党の候補者が選ばれる傾向があり、その政策は税金を引き下げて企業に利益を与え、移民に反対する傾向があります。

175

8 Congress (Capitol Hill)

The legislative branch of the government works in the Capitol, a building in Washington, D.C. The Capitol is also called the U.S. Capitol or the United States Capitol.

The Congress of the United States makes the federal laws of the United States.

Congress is composed of two parts: the Senate and the House of Representatives.

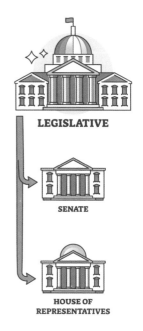

LEGISLATIVE

SENATE

HOUSE OF REPRESENTATIVES

There are 100 U.S. Senators, two from each state of the Union. Each senator represents all of the people of a state. Senators are elected to serve for six years.

There are 435 U.S. Representatives. Because Representatives are allotted in states according to population, states with a larger population have a larger number of Representatives. Each Representative represents the people of a Congressional district. Representatives are elected to serve for two years.

There is no limit on the number of terms that Senators and Representatives can serve.

議会（米国連邦議会、キャピトルヒル）

政府の立法府は、ワシントン D.C. にある Capitol（国会議事堂）という建物にあります。この Capitol は U.S. Capitol または United States Capitol とも呼ばれます。

米国連邦議会はアメリカの連邦法を制定します。

議会は上院と下院の2つの立法機関から成り立ちます。

上院には 100 名の議員が所属し、合衆国の各州から2名ずつ上院議員が選出されます。各上院議員はそれぞれの州の人々を代表します。上院議員の任期は6年です。

下院には 435 名の議員がいます。各州は人口に応じて下院議員数を割り当てられるため、人口が多い州には多くの下院議員がいます。各下院議員はそれぞれの選挙区の人々を代表します。下院議員の任期は2年です。

上院議員と下院議員の任期数に制限はありません。

Congress	
 The Senate	 The House of Representatives
100 seats 2 from each of the 50 states	435 seats According to the population ratio of the state
6 years	2 years

Let's try it!

Q16 Who makes federal laws?

Q17 What are the two parts of the U.S. Congress?

Q18 How many U.S. Senators are there?

Q19 We elect a U.S. Senator for how many years?

Q20 Who is one of your state's U.S. Senators now?

Q21 The House of Representatives has how many voting members?

Q22 We elect a U.S. Representative for how many years?

Q23 Name your U.S. Representative.

Q24 Who does a U.S. Senator represent?

Q25 Why do some states have more Representatives than other states?

Q47 What is the name of the Speaker of the House of Representatives now?

→ Answer p.203、205

議会	
上院	下院
100 名 50州から2名ずつ選出	**435 名** 州の人口比率によって割りふられる
6 年	**2 年**

Vocabulary

☐ Senator　上院議員　　　　　☐ Representative　下院議員
☐ district　地域

9 Making (Enacting) New Laws

When Congress wants to make a new law, it writes a document that is called a "bill." The Senate and the House of Representatives both have to pass the bill to approve it. If one or the other part of Congress vetoes (= votes against) it, the bill fails. If both bodies approve the bill, it then goes to the President.

If the President approves it, he or she signs the bill and it becomes a law. If the President does not approve it, the bill does not become a law.

In other words, the Senate, the House of Representatives, and the President have to approve of a bill in order for it to become a law.

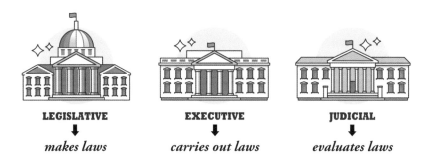

LEGISLATIVE
⬇
makes laws

EXECUTIVE
⬇
carries out laws

JUDICIAL
⬇
evaluates laws

⛅ Let's try it!

Q34 **Who vetoes bills?**

→ Answer p.205

　議会が新しく法律を成立させたいとき、"bill（法案）"と呼ばれる文書を作成します。そして上院および下院の両院が法案を可決する必要があります。もし上院または下院のどちらかで拒否された場合、法案は廃案となりますが、両院で承認されると、大統領に送られます。

　大統領が承認する場合、法案に署名し、法律となります。拒否権を行使する場合、法案は廃案となります。

　つまり、法案が法律になるには上院、下院、そして大統領が承認しなければならないのです。

Vocabulary

□ enact　実行する　　　　　□ approve　承認する
□ veto　反対票を投じる

10 Amendments

An amendment to the U.S. Constitution is more complex. Amendments are changes to the fundamental law of the nation, so they are extremely important. If an amendment passes Congress, it must then be ratified, within seven years, by 38 states before it can become part of the Constitution. Currently there are 27 amendments.

An example of this is the Equal Rights Amendment (ERA). In 1972 Congress passed the ERA. It was designed to guarantee equal legal rights to all American citizens regardless of gender. Supporters believed it would end legal discrimination between men and women in matters of divorce, child custody, property ownership, employment, and other matters. The ERA was quickly ratified by 35 states. But no additional states ratified the amendment. Because the required number of state governments did not ratify the amendment, it was rejected.

This ratification process is a way of balancing federal power and state power.

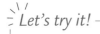 *Let's try it!*

Q7 **How many amendments does the U.S. Constitution have?**

→ Answer p.205

憲法の修正

　合衆国憲法の修正はより複雑です。修正条項は国の基本法を変更するものなので、非常に重要です。修正条項が議会を通過した場合、憲法の一部となるためには（実際に修正が成立するためには）7 年以内に 38 州で批准される必要があります。現在、27 の修正条項があります。

　この（プロセスの）一例が、1972 年に議会が可決した Equal Rights Amendment (ERA)、つまり男女平等憲法修正条項です。これは性別に関係なく、すべてのアメリカ国民に対し、法の下での権利の平等を保障するものでした。支持していた人々は、離婚や子どもの親権、財産所有、雇用などの問題で、法的な男女差別が終わると信じていました。ERA はただちに 35 州から批准されましたが、その後、他の州から批准されず、（憲法修正条項を成立させるために）必要な数の州議会の批准に満たなかったので、不成立となりました。

　この批准プロセスは連邦政府と州政府の権力を均衡にする方法なのです。

Vocabulary

- □ pass (Congress) （議会を）通過する
- □ regardless of ～にかかわらず
- □ divorce 離婚
- □ ratify 批准する
- □ discrimination 差別
- □ child custody 子どもの親権

11 The Supreme Court

The judicial branch of the federal government is the Supreme Court and the other lower federal courts. This branch reviews laws and explains the laws of the United States. Its duty is to resolve disagreements about the law and decide if the law goes against the Constitution.

The Supreme Court is the highest court in the United States. Its duty is to make a final review of the laws and decide if a law goes against the Constitution. This is the base of what we call the "rule of law."

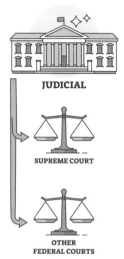

JUDICIAL

SUPREME COURT

OTHER FEDERAL COURTS

There are nine justices on the Supreme Court. They are appointed by the President and then must be approved by the Senate. These justices serve for life.

The head of the Supreme Court is the Chief Justice of the United States. The current Chief Justice is John Roberts (whose full name is John G. Roberts, Jr.).

Federal judges are nominated by the President and confirmed by the Senate.

Let's try it!

Q37 What does the judicial branch do?

Q38 What is the highest court in the United States?

Q39 How many justices are on the Supreme Court?

Q40 Who is the Chief Justice of the United States now?

→ Answer p.205

最高裁判所

連邦政府の司法府は最高裁判所およびその他の下級裁判所から成り立ちます。この部門は法律を審議し、法律について解明・説明します。法律についての見解の不一致を解決し、法律が憲法に反するか否かを判断する役割を果たします。

最高裁判所はアメリカにおける最上位の裁判所です。法律の最終審議をし、憲法に反するか否かを決断する役割を果たします。これが「法の支配」と呼ばれるものの基盤です。

最高裁判所は9名の裁判官で構成されます。大統領に任命され、上院による承認が必要です。任期は終身制です。

最高裁判所の長官は首席判事です。現在の首席判事はジョン・ロバーツ（フルネームはジョン・G・ロバーツ・ジュニア）です。

連邦判事は大統領によって指名され、上院で承認されます。

Vocabulary

☐ lower court　下級裁判所
☐ review of a law　法律の審議
☐ nominate　任命する

☐ resolve　解決する
☐ justice　裁判官
☐ confirm　承認する

12 Federal vs. State Government

In the United States, the national (federal) government and state governments have distinct powers and responsibilities. The Constitution says that the right to make a decision not given to the federal government is given to the state and local governments.

Federal government powers

- Print and mint money (currency and coins)
- Regulate interstate commerce (between states) and international trade
- Make treaties and conduct foreign policy
- Declare war
- Provide an army and navy
- Establish post offices
- Make laws necessary for carrying out these powers

State government powers

- Issue licenses (such as driver's licenses and business licenses)
- Regulate intrastate (= within the state) businesses
- Conduct elections
- Ratify amendments to the Constitution
- Promote public health and safety (for example, fire departments)
- Use powers established in the Constitution
- Establish schools

連邦政府 vs. 州政府

アメリカでは国家の政府（「連邦」政府）と州政府がそれぞれ異なる権限や責任を持っています。憲法では、連邦政府に付与されていない決定権は州政府や地方政府に与えられると定められています。

連邦政府の権限

- 紙幣を発行・貨幣を鋳造する（貨幣と硬貨）
- 州と州の間の通商（州際通商）と国際貿易を規制する
- 条約を結び、外交政策を行う
- 戦争を宣言する
- 陸軍・海軍を創設する
- 郵便局を設立する
- これらの権限を行使するために必要な法律を制定する

州政府の権限

- 免許証を発行する（運転免許証、営業許可証など）
- 州内（1つの州の中での）の事業を規制する
- 選挙を実施する
- 憲法の修正を批准する
- 公衆衛生と安全を促進する（例えば、消防署）
- 憲法で定められた権限を行使する
- 学校教育を提供する

- Collecting taxes
- Building roads
- Borrowing money
- Establishing courts
- Making and enforcing laws (police powers) and providing for public safety
- Chartering banks and corporations
- Spending money for general welfare

State governments

The government of each state is headed a Governor, who is elected by residents of the state. U.S. Territories also have a Governor. Washington, D.C., is not a state and it does not have a Governor.

⌣ *Let's try it!*

Q41 Under our Constitution, some powers belong to the federal government. What is one power of the federal government?

Q42 Under our Constitution, some powers belong to the states. What is one power of the states?

Q43 Who is the governor of your state now?

Q44 What is the capital of your state?

→ Answer p.207

連邦政府と州政府が共有する権限

- 税金の徴収
- 道路の建設
- お金を借りる
- 裁判所の設立
- 法律の制定および執行（警察の権限）、公共の安全の提供
- 銀行と企業の設立を許可
- 公共の福祉のためにお金を使う

州政府

　各州は州の住民によって選出される知事が率いています。アメリカ合衆国の海外領土にも知事がいます。ワシントン D.C. は州ではないため、知事がいません。

Vocabulary

☐ distinct　明確な、明確に異なる　　☐ currency　貨幣

☐ regulate　規制する、管理する　　☐ issue　発行する

☐ conduct　実施する　　☐ enforce　執行する

13 The Rights of Citizens

There are three important amendments to the U.S. Constitution about who can vote. One is that citizens eighteen and older can vote. The age was changed from 21 to 18 in 1971 during the Vietnam War. A second is that you do not have to pay a poll tax to vote. A third is that any citizen—men and women—can vote.

There are two rights that only U.S. citizens have. One is to vote in a federal election and another is to run for federal office in an election.

Everyone who lives in the United States has the following rights, which are included in the Bill of Rights:

Freedom of expression
Freedom of speech
Freedom of assembly
Freedom to petition the government
Freedom of religion
The right to bear arms

☀ Let's try it!

(Q10) **What is freedom of religion?**

(Q48) **There are several amendments to the Constitution about who can vote. Describe one of them.**

(Q50) **Name one right only for United States citizens.**

(Q51) **What are two rights of everyone living in the United States?**

(Q54) **How old do citizens have to be to vote for President?**

→ Answer p.207

市民の権利

　合衆国憲法には、投票権を持つ人に関する重要な修正条項が 3 つあります。1 つ目は、満 18 歳以上の市民が投票できるということです。その年齢は 1971 年のベトナム戦争中に 21 歳から 18 歳に変更になりました。2 つ目は、投票のためにお金（人頭税）を支払う必要はないということです。3 つ目は、男女を問わず、どの市民も投票できるということです。

　そして、アメリカ市民（国民）だけが持つ権利が 2 つあります。1 つは連邦選挙で投票することで、もう 1 つは連邦政府の公職に立候補することです。

　アメリカ合衆国に居住しているすべての人は、権利章典に含まれる次の権利を持っています。

　　表現の自由
　　言論の自由
　　集会の自由
　　政府に請願する自由
　　宗教の自由
　　武器を保有し携行する権利

Vocabulary

☐ amendment　修正　　　　　　　☐ poll tax　人頭税
☐ run for (election)　（選挙に）立候補する

---

14 The Responsibilities (Duties) of Citizens

People in the United States have a number of responsibilities. The fundamental responsibility is to obey the law. The basic principle of American democracy is the "rule of law," which means everyone must follow the laws. No one is above the law.

One responsibility of all male U.S. citizens and male immigrant non-citizens between the ages of 18 and 25 is to register with the Selective Service within 30 days of their 18th birthdays. Selective Service is a federal agency that keeps information regarding who might be up for a draft (conscription) into one of the U.S. Armed Forces. (In times of war or other emergency, when military personnel are required, this list of registrants is used to select personnel for service.) Failure to do this is breaking a law.

The military draft was suspended in 1973 at the end of the Vietnam War. However, all males have to register.

Military service is now voluntary. Because the military (Army, Navy, Air Force, Marines) does not discriminate by gender, skin color, educational background, or other prejudices, for some people it is an occupational choice. Joining one of the services is a way to earn a living, get education, and develop occupational skills.

市民の責任（義務）

　アメリカの人々にはいくつかの責任が課せられています。基本的な責任は法律に従うことです。アメリカの民主主義の原則は「法の支配」、つまりすべての人が法律に従わなければいけないということです。法を超越する者はいない（いかなる個人も法を超越した存在ではない）のです。

　18歳から25歳までのすべての男性アメリカ市民（国民）および男性移民（アメリカ籍を持たない・永住外国人）に課せられた責任の1つは、18歳の誕生日を迎えてから30日以内にセレクティブ・サービス・システム（選抜徴兵登録制度）に登録することです。セレクティブ・サービスは、アメリカ軍隊に招集（徴兵）する対象となる人についての情報を保持する連邦機関です（戦時や他の有事の際、この登録者リストを使って軍人を選抜し徴兵できるようにする）。これを怠ると、法律違反となります。

　徴兵制度はベトナム戦争後の1973年に廃止となりました。しかし、すべての男性は登録しなければいけません。

　現在、兵役は任意です。軍隊（陸軍、海軍、空軍、海兵隊）は性別、肌の色、学歴やその他の偏見によって差別しないため、人によっては職業の選択肢の1つでもあります。軍に入隊することは、生活費を稼ぎ、教育を受け、職業上のスキルを身につける方法の1つなのです。

Another responsibility is to pay taxes. Each citizen and non-citizen living in the United States is required to file federal income tax forms annually. The submission deadline is April 15 of each year. (Citizens and non-citizens in certain states are also required to file separate state income tax forms.)

In addition, every American citizen living outside the United States must also file an annual tax return and pay taxes to the federal government.

Other responsibilities are to serve on a jury and vote in national elections. Participation in these activities are both rights and responsibilities as citizens.

Let's try it!

Q49 What is one responsibility that is only for United States citizens?

Q56 When is the last day you can send in federal income tax forms?

Q57 When must all men register for the Selective Service?

→ Answer p.209

もう１つの責任（義務）は税金を納めることです。すべてのアメリカ市民およびアメリカに居住する非市民は、毎年、連邦所得税を申告する義務があります。提出期限は毎年の４月15日です（特定の州に居住するアメリカ市民および非市民は、別途、州の所得税申告書の提出が必要です）。

　さらに、米国外に居住しているすべてのアメリカ市民も毎年確定申告を行い、連邦政府に納税することが義務付けられています。

　この他には、陪審員を務め、連邦選挙で投票する責任があります。これらは権利でもあり、責任でもあります。

Vocabulary

☐ agency　機関、局
☐ tax form　確定申告書
☐ draft (conscription)　徴兵制度
☐ submission　提出

15 Participating in Democracy

The U.S. Constitution guarantees a number of right to citizens of the United States. It protects those rights and sets ways in which citizens can exercise those rights.

The obvious means for citizens to show their opinion is to vote in the election of candidates in local, state, and national elections. Citizens have the right to vote for someone who promotes their views in government. Citizens can become members of a political party that supports these candidates, and citizens can participate in the campaigns of their favorite candidate.

Citizens can also contact their state's Senators and Representatives and express their personal opinions on issues. A citizen also has the right to run for an elected office in their district or state.

In addition, if they feel a desire to carry out direct action, citizens are free to organize civic groups and community action groups. These groups publicly support or oppose issues or policies. They may also attempt to directly solve problems in their local community by cooperating with neighbors. Citizens many also write letters to the editor of local newspapers to express their opinions about local problems.

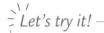
Let's try it!

> Q55) **What are two ways that Americans can participate in their democracy?**

→ Answer p.209

民主主義に参加する

合衆国憲法は、国民に多くの権利を保障しています。そしてこれらの権利を保護し、国民がその権利を行使する方法を定めています。

人々が自分の意見を示すための明白な手段は、地方選挙、州選挙、国政選挙において候補者に投票することです。国民は自分の意見を推進してくれる候補者に投票する権利を持ちます。候補者が所属する政党の会員になることができ、支持する候補者の選挙運動に参加することもできます。

また、自分の州の上院議員や下院議員に連絡を取り、問題に対する個人的な意見を表明することができます。自分の選挙区や州の選挙区に立候補する権利も持っています。

さらに、直接行動を起こしたいという気持ちがあれば、市民グループや地域活動グループを自由に組織し、公的に問題や政策を支持したり、反対したりできます。近隣の人々と協力して地域社会の問題を直接解決しようとすることも可能です。アメリカ国民は地元の新聞社に手紙を書き、地域の問題について自分の意見を表明することもできます。

16 The Oath of Allegiance

During the naturalization ceremonies in which successful applicants formally become citizens of the United States, they are required to recite this oath of allegiance to the United States. They stand and raise their right hand when they say the oath.

I hereby declare, on oath,

    that I absolutely and entirely renounce and abjure all allegiance and fidelity to any foreign prince, potentate, state, or sovereignty, of whom or which I have heretofore been a subject or citizen;

    that I will support and defend the Constitution and laws of the United States of America against all enemies, foreign and domestic;

    that I will bear true faith and allegiance to the same;

    that I will bear arms on behalf of the United States when required by the law;

    that I will perform noncombatant service in the Armed Forces of the United States when required by the law;

    that I will perform work of national importance under civilian direction when required by the law;

    and that I take this obligation freely without any mental reservation or purpose of evasion; so help me God.

Let's try it!

> **Q53** What is one promise you make when you become a United States citizen?

→ Answer p.209

忠誠の誓い

　市民権（帰化）の申請者が正式に市民権を得る市民権授与式では、このアメリカへの忠誠の誓いを復唱することが求められます。起立し、右手を上げて忠誠を誓います。

私はここに宣誓します

　これまで臣下または市民であった外国の王子、主権者、国家または主権に対するすべての忠誠と忠実を絶対的かつ完全に放棄および捨てることを

　国内外のすべての敵からアメリカ合衆国憲法およびアメリカ合衆国の法律を支持して守ることを

　これに真の信仰と忠誠を誓うことを

　法律によって求められた場合、合衆国を代表して武器を持つことを

　法律によって求められた場合、アメリカの軍隊で非戦闘員として務めることを

　法律によって求められた場合、民間の指示のもと国家への重要な仕事を執行することを

　そしてこの義務を、一切の心理的留保や回避の目的もなく、自由に引き受けると、神に誓います。

Let's Try Test Questions

Page 158

Q 12 What is the "rule of law"?

Page 160

Q 2 What does the Constitution do?

Q 3 The idea of self-government is in the first three words of the Constitution. What are these words?

Page 164

Q 1 What is the supreme law of the land?

Q 4 What is an amendment?

Q 5 What do we call the first ten amendments to the Constitution?

Q 6 What is one right or freedom from the First Amendment?

Page 166

Q 13 Name one branch or part of the government.

Q 14 What stops one branch of government from becoming too powerful?

Page 170

Q 15 Who is in charge of the executive branch?

Q 26 We elect a President for how many years?

Q 27 In what month do we vote for President?

Answers

A 12 「法の支配」とは何ですか？
Everyone must follow the law. すべての人が法律に従わなければいけない, **Leaders must obey the law.** 指導者は法律に従わなければいけない, **Government must obey the law.** 政府は法律に従わなければいけない, **No one is above the law.** いかなる個人も法律の上に立つことはできない（法を超越した存在ではない）

A 2 憲法の役割は何ですか？
Sets up the government 政府を組織する, **Defines the government** 政府（の権力）を定義する, **Protects basic rights of Americans** アメリカ国民の基本的権利を保障する

A 3 自治の概念は憲法の最初の 3 つの言葉に反映されています。この言葉は何ですか？
We the People （われら国民は）

A 1 アメリカ合衆国の最高法規は何ですか？
The Constitution 憲法

A 4 修正条項とは何ですか？
A change (to the Constitution) （憲法への）変更, **An addition (to the Constitution)** （憲法への）追加

A 5 憲法の修正条項の最初の 10 条は何と呼びますか？
The Bill of Rights 権利章典

A 6 修正条項の第 1 条に規定されている権利または自由を 1 つ挙げてください。
Speech 言論（の自由）, **Religion** 宗教（の自由）, **Assembly** 集会（の自由）, **Press** 出版（の自由）, **Petition the government** 請願（権）

A 13 アメリカ政府を構成する府または部分を 1 つ挙げてください。
Congress 議会, **The legislative branch** 立法府, **The President** 大統領, **The executive branch** 行政府, **The courts** 最高裁判所および下級裁判所, **The judicial branch** 司法府

A 14 1 つの部門に権力が集中しすぎないようにするものは何ですか？
Checks and balances チェックアンドバランス, **Separation of powers** 権力の分立（三権分立）

A 15 行政府の責任者は誰ですか？
The President 大統領

A 26 大統領の任期は何年ですか（大統領を選出するのは何年分ですか）？
Four (4) 4 年

A 27 大統領選挙は何月に行われますか？
November 11 月

Q 28 What is the name of the President of the United States now?

Q 29 What is the name of the Vice President of the United States now?

Q 30 If the President can no longer serve, who becomes President?

Q 31 If both the President and the Vice President can no longer serve, who becomes President?

Q 32 Who is the Commander-in-Chief of the military?

Q 33 Who signs bills to become laws?

Q 35 What does the President's Cabinet do?

Q 36 What are two Cabinet-level positions?

Q 45 What are the two major political parties in the United States?

Q 46 What is the political party of the President now?

Q 16 Who makes federal laws?

Q 17 What are the two parts of the U.S. Congress?

Q 18 How many U.S. Senators are there?

A 28 現在のアメリカ合衆国大統領の名前は何ですか？
Joe Biden ジョー・バイデン（2023 年現在）

A 29 現在のアメリカ合衆国副大統領の名前は何ですか？
Kamala Harris カマラ・ハリス（2023 年現在）

A 30 大統領が職務を遂行できなくなった場合、その地位を継承するのは誰ですか？
The Vice President 副大統領

A 31 大統領および副大統領が職務を遂行できなくなった場合、その地位を継承するのは誰ですか？
The Speaker of the House 下院議長

A 32 軍の最高司令官は誰ですか？
The President 大統領

A 33 法案に署名して法律として成立させるのは誰ですか？
The President 大統領

A 35 内閣（大統領顧問団）は何をするのですか？
Advises the President 大統領への助言

A 36 閣僚（省長官、行政各部長官）の役職を 2 つ挙げてください。
Secretary of Agriculture 農務長官 , **Secretary of Commerce** 商務長官 , **Secretary of Defense** 国防長官 , **Secretary of Education** 教育長官 , **Secretary of Energy** エネルギー長官 , **Secretary of Health and Human Services** 保健福祉長官 , **Secretary of Homeland Security** 国土安全保障長官 , **Secretary of Housing and Urban Development** 住宅都市開発長官 , **Secretary of the Interior** 内務長官 , **Secretary of Labor** 労働長官 , **Secretary of State** 国務長官 , **Secretary of Transportation** 運輸長官 , **Secretary of the Treasury** 財務長官 , **Secretary of Veterans Affairs** 退役軍人長官 , **Attorney General** 司法長官 , **Vice President** 副大統領

A 45 アメリカの 2 大政党は何ですか？
Democratic and Republican 民主党と共和党

A 46 現在の大統領が属する政党は何ですか？
Democratic Party 民主党（2023 年現在）

A 16 連邦法を作るのは誰ですか？
Congress 議会 , **Senate and House (of Representatives)** 上院（Senate）と下院（House of Representatives）, **(U.S. or national) legislature** （米国の）立法府

A 17 米国議会を構成する 2 つの部分は何ですか？
The Senate and House (of Representatives) 上院（Senate）と下院（House of Representatives）

A 18 上院議員の数は何名ですか？
One hundred (100) 100 名

Q 19 We elect a U.S. Senator for how many years?

Q 20 Who is one of your state's U.S. Senators now?

Q 21 The House of Representatives has how many voting members?

Q 22 We elect a U.S. Representative for how many years?

Q 23 Name your U.S. Representative.

Q 24 Who does a U.S. Senator represent?

Q 25 Why do some states have more Representatives than other states?

Q 47 What is the name of the Speaker of the House of Representatives now?

Q 34 Who vetoes bills?

Q 7 How many amendments does the U.S. Constitution have?

Q 37 What does the judicial branch do?

Q 38 What is the highest court in the United States?

Q 39 How many justices are on the Supreme Court?

Q 40 Who is the Chief Justice of the United States now?

Ⓐ19 上院議員の任期は何年ですか（上院議員を選出するのは何年分ですか）？
Six (6) 6 年

Ⓐ20 あなたの州の現在の上院議員の名前を 1 人挙げてください。
Answers will vary. 回答はそれぞれ異なります

Ⓐ21 下院に投票権を持つ議員は何名いますか？
Four hundred thirty-five (435) 435 名

Ⓐ22 下院議員の任期は何年ですか（下院議員を選出するのは何年分ですか）？
Two (2) 2 年

Ⓐ23 あなたの選挙区選出の下院議員の名前を挙げてください。
Answers will vary. 回答はそれぞれ異なります

Ⓐ24 上院議員は誰を代表するのですか？
All people of the state その州の全州民

Ⓐ25 一部の州で下院議員が他の州より多くいる理由は何ですか？
(Because of) the state's population その州の人口（のため），**(Because) they have more people** その州は（他の州より）人が多い（ため），**(Because) some states have more people** 一部の州は（他の州より）人が多い（ため）

Ⓐ47 現在の下院議長は誰ですか？
Kevin O. McCarthy ケビン・O・マッカーシー（2023 年現在）

Ⓐ34 法案に対して拒否権を行使するのは誰ですか？
The President 大統領

Ⓐ 7 合衆国憲法に修正条項はいくつありますか？
Twenty-seven (27)

Ⓐ37 司法府は何をするところですか？
Reviews laws 法律を審査する，**Explains laws** 法律について解明・説明する，**Resolves disputes (disagreements)** 争議（見解の不一致）を解決する，**Decides if a law goes against the Constitution** 法律が憲法に反するか否かを判断する

Ⓐ38 米国の最上位の裁判所は何ですか？
The Supreme Court 最高裁判所

Ⓐ39 現在、最高裁判所に最高裁判事は何名いますか？
9 justices 9 名

Ⓐ40 現在のアメリカ合衆国首席判事は誰ですか？
John G. Roberts, Jr. ジョン・G・ロバーツ・ジュニア（2023 年現在）

Q 41 Under our Constitution, some powers belong to the federal government. What is one power of the federal government?

Q 42 Under our Constitution, some powers belong to the states. What is one power of the states?

Q 43 Who is the governor of your state now?

Q 44 What is the capital of your state?

Q 10 What is freedom of religion?

Q 48 There are several amendments to the Constitution about who can vote. Describe one of them.

Q 50 Name one right only for United States citizens.

Q 51 What are two rights of everyone living in the United States?

Q 54 How old do citizens have to be to vote for President?

A 41　憲法の下では、いくつかの権限は連邦政府に属しています。連邦政府の権限を１つ挙げてください。

To print money 紙幣を発行する , **To declare war** 戦争を宣言する , **To create an army** 軍隊を創設する , **To make treaties** 条約を結ぶ

A 42　憲法の下では、いくつかの権限は州に属しています。州の権限を１つ挙げてください。

Provide schooling and education 学校教育を提供する , **Provide protection (police)** 保護を提供する（警察）, **Provide safety (fire departments)** 安全を提供する（消防署）, **Give a driver's license** 運転免許証を発行する , **Approve zoning and land use** 区域分けや土地利用を承認する

A 43　あなたが住んでいる州の知事は誰ですか？

Answers will vary. (District of Columbia residents should answer that D.C. does not have a governor.) 回答はそれぞれ異なります（コロンビア特別区の住民は、知事がいないと回答する）

A 44　あなたが住んでいる州の州都はどこですか？

Answers will vary. (District of Columbia residents should answer that D.C. is not a state and does not have a capital. Residents of U.S. territories should name the capital of the territory.) 回答はそれぞれ異なります（コロンビア特別区（D.C.）は州ではないため、その地区の住人は 州都がないと回答するべきです。アメリカ合衆国の海外領土の住民は、その領土の州都を回答します）

A 10　宗教の自由とは何ですか？

You can practice any religion, or not practice a religion. 宗教上の信念を選択する、あるいは宗教を持たない権利

A 48　憲法には投票権を持つ者に関するいくつかの修正条項があります。その１つを挙げてください。

Citizens eighteen and older (can vote). 満 18 歳以上の市民（が投票できる）, **You don't have to pay (a poll tax) to vote.** 投票のためにお金を払う（人頭税を支払う）必要はない , **Any citizen can vote. (Women and men of any race can vote.)** どの市民も投票できる（人種を問わず女性と男性両方が投票できる）

A 50　アメリカ市民（国民）だけが持つ権利を１つ挙げてください。

Vote in a federal election 連邦選挙で投票すること , **Run for federal office** 連邦政府の公職に立候補すること

A 51　アメリカ合衆国に居住しているすべての人が持つ権利を２つ挙げてください。

Freedom of expression 表現の自由 , **Freedom of speech** 言論の自由 , **Freedom of assembly** 集会の自由 , **Freedom to petition the government** 政府に請願する自由 , **Freedom of religion** 宗教の自由 , **The right to bear arms** 武器を保有し携行する権利

A 54　市民（国民）が大統領選挙に投票できるのは何歳からですか？

Eighteen and older 18 歳以上

Page 194

Q 49 What is one responsibility that is only for United States citizens?

Q 56 When is the last day you can send in federal income tax forms?

Q 57 When must all men register for the Selective Service?

Page 196

Q 55 What are two ways that Americans can participate in their democracy?

Page 198

Q 53 What is one promise you make when you become a United States citizen?

A49　アメリカ市民（国民）だけに課せられた責任を 1 つ挙げてください。

Serve on a jury 陪審員を務めること , **Vote in a federal election** 連邦選挙で投票すること

A56　連邦所得税申告書の提出期限はいつですか？

April 15 4 月 15 日

A57　すべての男性がセレクティブ・サービス・システム（選抜徴兵登録制度）への登録が義務付けられているのはいつ（何歳）ですか？

At age 18 18 歳になったら , **Between 18 and 25** 18 歳から 25 歳までの間

A55　アメリカ人が民主主義に参加できる例を 2 つ挙げてください。

Vote 投票する , **Join a political party** 政党に参加する , **Help with a campaign** 選挙運動を手伝う , **Join a civic group** 市民団体に加入する , **Join a community group** 地域グループに参加する , **Give an elected official your opinion on an issue** 公職に任命された人に問題などについて意見を伝える , **Call Senators and Representatives** 上院議員や下院議員に電話をする , **Publicly support or oppose an issue or policy** 問題や政策に対して公に支援または反対する , **Run for office** 公職に立候補する , **Write to a newspaper** 新聞に投書する

A53　新たにアメリカ合衆国市民となる人が（忠誠の誓いで）約束するものを 1 つ挙げてください。

Give up loyalty to other countries 他国への忠誠を放棄すること , **Defend the Constitution and laws of the United States** 合衆国憲法と法を守ること , **Obey the laws of the United States** アメリカ合衆国の法律に従うこと , **Serve in the U.S. military (if needed)** アメリカ軍の兵役に従事すること（必要な場合）, **Serve (do important work for) the nation (if needed)** 国に奉仕すること（必要な場合）, **Be loyal to the United States** アメリカ合衆国に忠誠であること

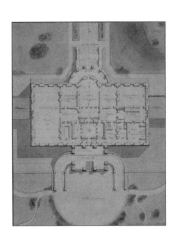

The White House Washington, D.C.
Site plan and principal story plan., 1807.

Part 4

Understanding
the U.S. Better

アメリカをもっと理解するために

1 Volunteering and Community Service

When social problems have grown serious and there are few government programs to help, citizens have often tried to help people who are less fortunate. In 1889, Jane Addams opened Hull House, a settlement house in a poor part of Chicago, Illinois. It became a community center, providing food and shelter, medical services, and child care for working mothers. The hungry could get a nutritious hot meal, and the unemployed could get help in finding a job. Hull House also helped newly arrived immigrants make the difficult transition to life in urban America.

Volunteering to help the needy—often complete strangers—continues to be common in the United States. These activities can be started by church groups, friends and acquaintances, and even social media connections. Participants donate time and energy to meet many different kinds of needs.

One common volunteer activity is collecting used clothing, cleaning it, and making it available to anyone who needs it. Another is gathering donations of leftover food items from restaurants and preparing meals at "community kitchens" for anyone who needs a free meal.

Volunteers may also gather canned goods, packaged foods, and daily necessities at "food banks" in churches and other available spaces, where needy families can pick them up.

ボランティアと社会奉仕活動

社会問題が深刻化したにもかかわらず、政府による支援が不十分であるとき、アメリカの市民は苦境にいる人々に手を差し伸べようとしてきました。1889年、ジェーン・アダムスはイリノイ州シカゴの貧しい地域にセツルメントハウスであるハルハウスを設立しました。 ここは食料と住居、医療サービス、そして働く母親には保育を提供するコミュニティセンターとなりました。飢えている人は栄養価の高い温かい食事をとることができ、失業者は仕事を見つけるための支援を受けることができました。 また、ハルハウスはアメリカに到着したばかりでアメリカ都市部での生活に慣れるのに苦労していた移民たちもサポートしました。

今もアメリカでは、多くの場合は赤の他人であるにもかかわらず、困窮した状況に置かれた人々を支援するボランティアが一般的となっています。これらの活動は、教会のグループ、友人や知人、さらにはソーシャルメディアのつながりがきっかけで始まることもあります。 参加者は、様々な要望を満たすために時間とエネルギーを「寄付」します。

典型的なボランティアとして、古着を集め、洗濯して必要な人に提供する活動が挙げられます。 もう1つの例は、レストランで残った食料品を寄付してもらい、それらを調理して「コミュニティキッチン」で食事を必要とする人々に無料で提供することです。

また、缶詰、加工食品や日用品を集めて、教会やその他の利用可能な場所に「フードバンク」を設置し、生活に困窮している家族はそれらを無料で持ち帰ることができます。

2 School Education

Schools may be divided into elementary (grades 1-6), junior high (7-9), and high school (10-12) or into elementary (grades 1-5), middle school (6-8), and high school (9-12).

Borrowing from college designations, grade 9 is often called "freshman in high school," grade 10 is "sophomore in high school," grade 11 is "junior in high school," and grade 12 is called "senior in high school."

The school systems of America are not dependent on the Department of Education in the way that Japanese schools operate under the guidelines of the Ministry of Education. The school systems are primarily under the local guidance and control of the states and municipalities. This has several implications.

Each state has a different school administration system, and the textbooks are chosen by the state or by the municipality. When families move from state to state their children may have completely different textbooks and curriculum. This has caused some education specialists to call for a basic "core knowledge" curriculum for all of the states.

The states are also different in mandatory school entering ages and compulsory education ages. Some states do not require school attendance after a student turns 16. Others require attendance to the age of 18. Some states only require attendance through grade 10.

学校教育

学校は小学校 (1-6 年生)、中学校 (7-9 年生)、高校 (10-12 年生)、または小学校 (1-5 年生)、中学校 (6-8 年生)、高校 (9-12 年生) に分かれます。

大学の学年の呼び方を用いて、9 年生は「ハイスクール・フレッシュマン」、10 年生は「ハイスクール・ソフモア」、11 年生は「ハイスクール・ジュニア」、12 年生は「ハイスクール・シニア」と呼ばれることがよくあります。

アメリカの学校制度は、日本の学校が文科省のガイドラインに基づいて運営されているのと同じようには教育省の影響を受けません。学校制度は主に州や地方自治体の指導および管理下にあります。これは次のようなことを意味します。

各州にはそれぞれの異なる学校運営システムがあり、州または地方自治体が教科書を選びます。ある州から別の州に引っ越す家族の子どもたちは、まったく異なるカリキュラムの学校で、異なる教科書を使用することになる可能性があります。このことから、一部の教育専門家は、すべての州で共通する、基本となる「コア知識」のカリキュラムを求めるようになりました。

さらに、義務教育の入学年齢や義務教育の対象年齢も州によって異なります。一部の州では、16 歳になった生徒にはそれ以降の学校への出席を義務付けていません。別の州では 18 歳までは出席が義務付けられています。また一部の州では 10 年生の終わりまでの出席のみが必須となっています。

3 School Systems

Until the 1950s, states in the South carried out policies of "separate but equal" in the public schools. Black kids went to one school and white kids went to another school. The state governments claimed that they gave children equal quality education, but, of course, the white kids received better conditions, teachers, equipment, and textbooks. The Supreme Court declared that "separate but equal" was against the Constitution, so race is not supposed to be a factor.

However, if a school is in a Black neighborhood, its students will be mostly Black. And if that neighborhood pays low taxes, the schools will have less money to support school education. As a result, the students in these schools will have lower quality facilities and lower paid teachers. Children—of all colors—who live in higher-income neighborhoods will benefit by going to schools with better equipment and higher paid teachers.

Schools budgets are supplied by the state government budget with some federal subsidies. States can attract businesses and factories by offering low tax rates. This may increase jobs, but it has a negative impact on school budgets. There is less money to pay teachers and to buy essential equipment for the schools.

学校制度

1950年代まで、南部の州は公立学校において「分離されているが平等」という政策を実施していました。 黒人の子どもたちと白人の子どもたちは別々の学校に通いました。 州政府は、子どもたちに同等の質の教育を与えていると主張しましたが、当然のことながら、白人の子どもたちにはより良い教育環境や教師、設備、そして教科書が提供されました。最高裁判所が「分離されているが平等」は憲法に違反していると宣言したように、人種がこのような違いに影響する要素となるべきではありません。

しかし、ある学校が黒人の住む地域にある場合、その学校に通う生徒のほとんどが黒人になります。また、その地域の市民による納税額が低い場合、学校教育にかける資金が少なくなります。その地域の子どもたちは設備の質が低く、低賃金の教師がいる学校に通うことになります。人種に関係なく、高所得層が暮らす地域に住む子どもたちは、より良い設備が整い、より高給の教師が雇われている学校に通うことになり、多くの恩恵を受けられます。

学校の予算は州政府の予算と一部の連邦補助金によって賄われています。州は低い税率によって企業や工場を誘致することができます。 これによって雇用は増えるかもしれませんが、学校の予算には悪影響を与える可能性があります。教師の給料や、設備投資の予算が減ってしまうのです。

4 Religion

One of the more dependable sources on American religious beliefs is carried out by the Pew Research Center, which regularly surveys the religious beliefs of the U.S. population.

Although Christians continue to make up a majority of the population, they are shrinking in number. A decade ago some 75% of Americans told surveys that they were "Christian." Currently (2023) that figure has dropped to 63%. Close to one third of American adults say that they have "no affiliation" with any religion at all, and that percentage is rising.

When a person says he or she is "Christian," what does that mean?

Roughly one-third of American adults now say that they *seldom or never pray.* This is an increase of 18% who said this in 2007.

The recent Pew survey asked how important religion is in their lives. A decade ago 56% said religion was *very important* in their lives. In the recent survey that number has dropped to 41%.

How often do American adults attend religious services? The survey says that 31% attend once a month. In contrast, 26% seldom attend and 27% never attend.

In short, religion is becoming less important, fewer people are praying, and fewer are attending a religious service.

宗教

アメリカの宗教的信念に関して、アメリカ国民の宗教的信念を定期的に調査しているピューリサーチセンターは信頼できる情報源の1つです。

キリスト教徒は引き続き人口の大部分を占めていますが、その数は減少しています。10年前の調査では、アメリカ人の約75％が自分は「クリスチャン」であると答えていました。現在（2023年）、その数字は63％に減っています。アメリカの成人人口の3分の1近くがどの宗教も「まったく信仰していない」と答えており、その割合は増加しています。

人が自分を「クリスチャン」だと言うとき、それは何を意味するのでしょうか。

現在、アメリカの成人人口の約3分の1は、ほとんど祈りを捧げない、あるいはまったく祈らないと述べています。このような人の数は2007年と比較すると18％増加しています。

また、最近のピュー調査では、生活のなかでの宗教の重要性について尋ねました。10年前は56％の人が、宗教は人生において非常に重要だと答えていました。最近の調査では、その数字は41％まで減少しました。

アメリカの成人はどれくらいの頻度で宗教行事（礼拝）に出席するのでしょうか。調査によると、31％の人が月に1回参加していると答えました。それに対して、26％はほとんど出席せず、27％は一切出席しないと回答しました。

つまり、宗教の重要性が薄れ、祈る人も減り、礼拝に参加する人も減っているのです。

5 Gun Regulations

America is unfortunately unique in the high number of crimes involving guns. In the background of this serious problem is the Bill of Rights, the first ten amendments of the United States Constitution.

During the American Revolution, the colonies did not have a regular army. Volunteers with their own weapons gathered to fight against the British army of full-time, trained soldiers. After the colonists defeated the British, won their independence, and composed the Constitution, they added ten Amendments that are especially important regarding weapons.

The Second Amendment guarantees "the right to bear arms"— "arms" meaning weapons. The newly born United States of America did not have a regular army, so this amendment allowed the right to own a gun within the context of serving in a "militia," a force that is raised from a *civilian* population *in an emergency*. Such militias were intended to be *state militias*, not a national army, to provide national security.

Americans are roughly divided into two groups. One group clings to the Second Amendment phrase "right to bear arms," taking that as a Constitutional right. This group holds that the federal government has no right "take away their arms." The other group claims, rightly, that gun control is not against the Constitution and is essential to making America a safer place.

銃規制

　残念なことにアメリカは、銃犯罪が多いという点において独特です。この深刻な問題の背景には、合衆国憲法修正条項の最初の10条である「権利章典」があります。

　アメリカ独立戦争中、植民地には正規軍がありませんでした。訓練を受けた正規兵士からなるイギリス軍と戦うため、それぞれの武器を持った志願兵が集結したのです。植民地人がイギリスを破り、独立を勝ち取り、憲法を制定した後に、武器に関して特に重要となる10の修正条項を追加しました。

　憲法修正第2条は、「武器を保有し携行する権利」を保障しています。新しく誕生したアメリカ合衆国には正規軍がなかったため、この修正により、緊急時に民間人から招集した部隊である「民兵」に服するという文脈で銃を所有する権利が認められたのです。このような民兵は、国軍ではなく、国家の安全を提供するための州民兵であることが意図されていました。

　アメリカ人は大きく2つのグループに分けられます。1つは憲法修正第2条の「武器を保有し携行する権利」という文言に固執し、それを憲法上の権利だと解釈している人々です。連邦政府に対して、「武器を取り上げる」権利はないと主張しています。もう一方のグループは、銃規制は憲法に違反しておらず、アメリカをより安全な場所にするために不可欠であると正当に主張しています。

100 Civics Questions for the Naturalization Test

国籍取得テストのための 100 題

Answer

1 **What is the supreme law of the land?**
アメリカ合衆国の最高法規は何ですか？
→ p.201

2 **What does the Constitution do?**
憲法の役割は何ですか？
→ p.201

3 **The idea of self-government is in the first three words of the Constitution. What are these words?**
自治の概念は憲法の最初の３つの言葉に反映されています。この言葉は何ですか？
→ p.201

4 **What is an amendment?**
修正条項とは何ですか？
→ p.201

5 **What do we call the first ten amendments to the Constitution?**
憲法の修正条項の最初の 10 条は何と呼びますか？
→ p.201

6 **What is one right or freedom from the First Amendment?**
修正条項の第 1 条に規定されている権利または自由を 1 つ挙げてください。
→ p.201

7 **How many amendments does the U.S. Constitution have?**
合衆国憲法に修正条項はいくつありますか？
→ p.205

8 **What did the Declaration of Independence do?**
独立宣言は何をしましたか？
→ p.73

9 **What are two rights in the Declaration of Independence?**
独立宣言に述べられている権利を２つ挙げてください。
→ p.73

10 **What is freedom of religion?**
宗教の自由とは何ですか？
→ p.207

36 **What are two Cabinet-level positions?**
閣僚（省長官、行政各部長官）の役職を２つ挙げてください。
→ p.203

37 **What does the judicial branch do?**
司法府は何をするのですか？
→ p.205

38 **What is the highest court in the United States?**
米国の最上位の裁判所は何ですか？
→ p.205

39 **How many justices are on the Supreme Court?**
現在、最高裁判所に最高裁判事は何名いますか？
→ p.205

40 **Who is the Chief Justice of the United States now?**
現在のアメリカ合衆国首席判事は誰ですか？
→ p.205

41 **Under our Constitution, some powers belong to the federal government. What is one power of the federal government?**
憲法の下では、いくつかの権限は連邦政府に属しています。連邦政府の権限を１つ挙げてください。
→ p.207

42 **Under our Constitution, some powers belong to the states. What is one power of the states?**
憲法の下では、いくつかの権限は州に属しています。州の権限を１つ挙げてください。
→ p.207

43 **Who is the governor of your state now?**
あなたが住んでいる州の知事は誰ですか？
→ p.207

44 **What is the capital of your state?**
あなたが住んでいる州の州都はどこですか？
→ p.207

45 **What are the two major political parties in the United States?**
アメリカの二大政党は何ですか？
→ p.203

46 **What is the political party of the President now?**
現在の大統領が属する政党は何ですか？
→ p.203

47 **What is the name of the Speaker of the House of Representatives now?**
現在の下院議長は誰ですか？
→ p.205

48 There are several amendments to the Constitution about who can vote. Describe one of them.
→ p.207
憲法には投票権を持つ者に関するいくつかの修正条項があります。その1つを挙げてください。

49 What is one responsibility that is only for United States citizens?
→ p.209
アメリカ市民（国民）だけに課せられた責任を1つ挙げてください。

50 Name one right only for United States citizens.
→ p.207
アメリカ市民（国民）だけが持つ権利を1つ挙げてください。

51 What are two rights of everyone living in the United States?
→ p.207
アメリカ合衆国に居住しているすべての人が持つ権利を2つ挙げてください。

52 What do we show loyalty to when we say the Pledge of Allegiance?
→ p.47
忠誠宣言を唱える際、何に対して忠誠を誓うのですか？

53 What is one promise you make when you become a United States citizen?
→ p.209
新たにアメリカ合衆国市民となる人が（忠誠の誓いで）約束するものを1つ挙げてください。

54 How old do citizens have to be to vote for President?
→ p.207
市民（国民）が大統領選挙に投票できるのは何歳からですか？

55 What are two ways that Americans can participate in their democracy?
→ p.209
アメリカ人が民主主義に参加できる例を2つ挙げてください。

56 When is the last day you can send in federal income tax forms?
→ p.209
連邦所得税申告書の提出期限はいつですか？

57 When must all men register for the Selective Service?
→ p.209
すべての男性がセレクティブ・サービス・システム（選抜徴兵登録制度）への登録が義務付けられているのはいつ（何歳）ですか？

58 What is one reason colonists came to America?
→ p.73
入植者がアメリカに来た理由の1つを挙げてください。

59 Who lived in America before the Europeans arrived?
→ p.73
ヨーロッパ人が到着する前のアメリカには誰が住んでいましたか？

60 What group of people was taken to America and sold as slaves?
アメリカへ連れ去られて奴隷として売られたのはどの人々ですか？
→ p.73

61 Why did the colonists fight the British?
入植者はなぜイギリスと戦ったのですか?
→ p.73

62 Who wrote the Declaration of Independence?
独立宣言を書いたのは誰ですか？
→ p.73

63 When was the Declaration of Independence adopted?
独立宣言が採択されたのはいつですか？
→ p.73

64 There were 13 original states. Name three.
独立した当初は 13 の州がありました。そのうち 3 州を挙げてください。
→ p.97

65 What happened at the Constitutional Convention?
憲法制定会議では何が起きましたか？
→ p.97

66 When was the Constitution written?
憲法が書かれたのはいつですか?
→ p.97

67 The Federalist Papers supported the passage of the U.S. Constitution. Name one of the writers.
『ザ・フェデラリスト』はアメリカ合衆国憲法の成立を支援しました。その執筆者を1名挙げてください。
→ p.97

68 What is one thing Benjamin Franklin is famous for?
ベンジャミン・フランクリンはどのようなことで有名ですか?その1つを挙げてください。
→ p.97

69 Who is the "Father of Our Country"?
「建国の父」は誰ですか?
→ p.97

70 Who was the first President?
初代アメリカ合衆国大統領は誰ですか？
→ p.97

71 What territory did the United States buy from France in 1803?
アメリカ合衆国が 1803 年にフランスから購入した領土はどこですか？
→ p.127

72 Name one war fought by the United States in the 1800s.
アメリカが 1800 年代に戦った戦争を 1 つ挙げてください。
→ p.127

73 Name the U.S. war between the North and the South.
アメリカの北（北軍）と南（南軍）が戦った戦争の名前を挙げてください。
→ p.127

74 Name one problem that led to the Civil War.
南北戦争を引き起こした問題を1つ挙げてください。
→ p.127

75 What was one important thing that Abraham Lincoln did?
エイブラハム・リンカーンが行った重要なことの1つを挙げてください。
→ p.127

76 What did the Emancipation Proclamation do?
奴隷解放宣言は何をしましたか？
→ p.127

77 What did Susan B. Anthony do?
スーザン・B・アンソニーは何をした人物ですか？
→ p.127

78 Name one war fought by the United States in the 1900s.
アメリカ合衆国が 1900 年代に戦った戦争を1つ挙げてください。
→ p.155

79 Who was President during World War Ⅰ ?
第一次世界大戦中の大統領は誰でしたか?
→ p.155

80 Who was President during the Great Depression and World War II?
大恐慌と第二次世界大戦時の大統領は誰でしたか？
→ p.155

81 Who did the United States fight in World War II?
アメリカは第二次世界大戦で誰と戦いましたか？
→ p.155

82 Before he was President, [Dwight] Eisenhower was a general. What war was he in?
（ドワイト）アイゼンハワーは大統領就任前では司令官でした。どの戦争の司令官でしたか？
→ p.155

83 During the Cold War, what was one main concern of the United States?
冷戦中にアメリカが主に懸念していたことの1つを挙げてください。
→ p.155

84 What movement tried to end racial discrimination?
人種差別を終わらせようとした運動は何ですか？
→ p.155

98 **What is the name of the national anthem?**
国歌の名前は何ですか？ → p.47

99 **When do we celebrate Independence Day?**
独立記念日はいつですか？ → p.47

100 **Name two national U.S. holidays.**
アメリカの祝日を２つ挙げてください。 → p.47

著者紹介

ジェームス・M・バーダマン

早稲田大学名誉教授。1947年アメリカ・テネシー州生まれ。プリンストン神学校教育専攻、修士。ハワイ大学大学院アジア研究専攻、修士。専門はアメリカ文化史。著書に『毎日の英文法』『地図で読むアメリカ』（朝日新聞出版）、『日英対訳 世界に紹介したい日本の100人』（山川出版社）、『アメリカ黒人史』『英語の処方箋』（ちくま新書）、『ネイティブが教える 日本人が絶対間違える英語大全』(KADOKAWA)、『3つの基本ルール＋αで英語の冠詞はここまで簡単になる』（アルク）、『英語でお悔やみ申し上げます - 冠婚葬祭・非常時の英語表現』（ベレ出版）など多数。

マヤ・バーダマン

上智大学卒業。ハワイ大学留学。外資系企業に勤務し、医学英語に携わる。著書に『英語のお手本 そのままマネしたい「敬語」集』『英語の気配り マネしたい「マナー」と「話し方」』（朝日新聞出版）、『品格のある英語は武器になる』（宝島社）、『外資系1年目のための英語の教科書』(KADOKAWA)、『人を動かす、気配りの英語表現』（ジャパンタイムズ出版）、『医学英語のお手本』（丸善出版）などがある。

http://www.jmvardaman.com/

- ● ── DTP　　　　清水康広（WAVE）
- ● ── 校正　　　　余田 志保
- ● ── 装丁　　　　上坊 菜々子
- ● ── 装画　　　　Studio-Takeuma
- ● ── 本文イラスト　いげた めぐみ

アメリカ国籍取得テストでアメリカの一般教養と英語を学ぶ

2023 年 8 月 25 日	初版発行
2023 年 11 月 4 日	第 2 刷発行

著者	ジェームス・M・バーダマン　マヤ・バーダマン
発行者	内田 真介
発行・発売	ベレ出版
	〒162-0832　東京都新宿区岩戸町12 レベッカビル TEL.03-5225-4790 FAX.03-5225-4795 ホームページ　https://www.beret.co.jp/
印刷	三松堂印刷株式会社
製本	根本製本株式会社

ISBN 978-4-86064-735-3 C2082　　　　　　　　　　編集担当　新谷友佳子